TACKLING TOXICITY

A SKILL-BASED GUIDE TO ADDRESSING TOXICITY

TACKLING TOXICITY

A SKILL-BASED GUIDE TO ADDRESSING TOXICITY

Mauricio A. Velásquez, MBA
Founder, President
Diversity Training Group

MANUSCRIPTS
PRESS

COPYRIGHT © 2024 MAURICIO A. VELÁSQUEZ
All rights reserved.

TACKLING TOXICITY
A Skill-Based Guide to Addressing Toxicity

ISBN   979-8-88926-234-3   *Paperback*
               979-8-88926-235-0   *Hardcover*
               979-8-88926-233-6   *Digital Ebook*

I dedicate this book to my family: my Colombian immigrant parents Antonio and Irma Velásquez who came to this country to forge a better life and taught me early on to work hard and persevere and "don't let anyone tell you you are inferior or less than anyone else."

I also dedicate this book to my immediate family—Kelly my bride and our children Ethan, Elise, and Maya—who taught me to be a better husband and father and who motivated me—drove me—to write this book for a better workplace and a better society.

"For the silent sufferers, the targets of toxic behaviors who seek skills, tools, and knowledge to free themselves from their toxic situations and environments."

— *MV*

CONTENTS

	INTRODUCTION	11
CHAPTER 1.	THE TOXIC PERSON AND THEIR BEHAVIORS	17
CHAPTER 2.	HOW UNAWARE ARE YOU? NARCISSISM AT ITS BEST!	29
CHAPTER 3.	ANGER MANAGEMENT— KNOW YOUR TRIGGERS	45
CHAPTER 4.	THE CEO GRABBER— DRUNK WITH POWER	55
CHAPTER 5.	HOME FRONT HAS BECOME MORE TOXIC	71
CHAPTER 6.	WORKPLACE RIDDLED WITH TOXICITY	91
CHAPTER 7.	FROM BYSTANDER TO UPSTANDER— IN ALL ASPECTS OF YOUR LIFE, SPORTS FOR STARTERS	107
CHAPTER 8.	CHIEF OF FIRE DEPARTMENT, CHIEF OF TOXICITY	127
CHAPTER 9.	LIVING THE AMERICAN DREAM— SOME TOXIC FOLKS TRY TO RUIN IT	135
CHAPTER 10.	COACH HIM BUT WE CAN'T FIRE HIM	145
CHAPTER 11.	THINK LIKE A WORKPLACE INVESTIGATOR	159
CHAPTER 12.	GOING BACK INTO THE WORLD WITH YOUR EYES AND EARS WIDE OPEN	171

INTERVIEWS	185
WEBSITE/ARTICLES—ADDITIONAL RESOURCES	195
ACKNOWLEDGMENTS	199
NOTES	201

INTRODUCTION

"Toxic people take up most, if not all, of my time."

As a diversity and inclusion trainer, I hear this comment a lot. Most people can recognize toxic behavior as it's happening in their lives. I have been around toxic employees, toxic environments, toxic family members, toxic students, and toxic friends my whole life.

In the summer of 2018, I led a Diversity, Inclusion, and Respectful Workplace training for a major utility company. I was setting up the projector and the screen, putting up easel paper, and arranging chairs when a man tapped me on the shoulder.

"Are you our trainer today?" he asked. "Can I talk to you for a minute?" I looked down at my watch. He was an hour and fifteen minutes early for the training. "I came early to talk to you." As a trainer and facilitator (of more than twenty-two years at this point in my career), I picked up on his nonverbal cues and body language—he was agitated.

I smiled. "What's up?" I asked. "How can I help you?" I invited him to sit at the first row of tables.

He sat down and immediately went into a passionate and emotional plea. "You know I think this workshop is a bunch of crap. My boss insisted I be at the first workshop offered at this site and so here I am. But I don't want to be here, I don't need this class."

I looked him right in the eyes. "Wow, you came early to let me have it." I smiled. He didn't.

"Listen," he grumbled, "just let me sign the roster and I'll be on my way out of here before anyone else arrives."

I asked if he'd spoken to anyone in advance about the workshop or reviewed the materials. He hadn't. "You have no idea what my workshop is about, but you know you don't need it?" I pulled up a slide in my presentation of three concentric circles. "This smallest, innermost circle is *what you know*. The next circle represents *what you don't know*. And this large outer circle is *what you don't know you don't know*. Unless you attend my workshop, you won't know what you don't know."

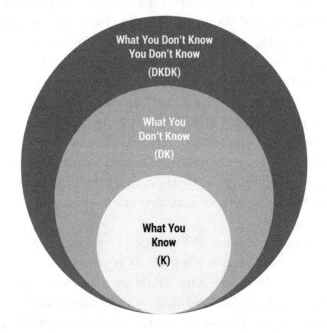

He wasn't impressed. "I don't give a flying *&$% what we are doing today!"

I looked at him and said with glee, "You are fantastic!" He was very confused. I continued. "You have a bias about a workshop on bias. You're being very difficult about a workshop that teaches our participants how to deal with difficult people. You're the reason I get this work."

I did not let him sign the roster and leave. He sat in the front row for the entire training. He didn't participate at first, but by the time I got to the content on toxic employees, he looked at me with wide eyes, as if he was saying *This is me, isn't it*? At the end of the training, he signed the roster, with his back to me as he was walking out, and he said, "Thanks for making me stay." I returned several times but he never, ever spoke to me again.

As I packed up the room, the client who'd hired me asked, "Did our friend come early and let you have it?"

"Wait," I said. "You knew this was going to happen and didn't warn me?"

"What's the fun in that?" she replied, grinning. "I didn't want to ruin the surprise!"

In my profession, I am constantly thrown into the middle of toxic situations—and I love it. I love going into the middle of an employee relations hurricane. No pain, no gain. I learned early in life that if you don't deal with issues while they are small and manageable, they can get out of control like a brushfire turned wildfire. Often, my clients have waited too long, and then bring me in when it is nearly an unmanageable situation.

I am the first-born son of immigrant parents. Culturally, it is my duty to be the problem-solver, the coach, and the conflict-resolver. My younger siblings recognize the role

I play in our family and oblige to "let Mauricio deal with it." Being on the front lines of all family conflicts put me in many toxic situations. I became a good listener, one that empathizes but can also detach. I enjoy listening to others, advising, and helping people solve their problems and resolve conflict.

I continue to be hired to run head-first into difficult situations in my career. There are not many Hispanic or Latino diversity trainers in the country, so I am very busy when you look at the emerging demographics in the workplace and marketplace. I am also one of the few male sexual harassment prevention trainers and consultants in the country. I get "race work" because I am not Black or African American (making me neutral?). I get "gender work" because I am a man. "Our people will not listen to a woman" (gender bias about the trainer). My mentor, Linda Shevitz, taught me much of what I know. Yet, she can present the same content I do and be written off as a "radical feminist." It's frustrating.

If you are the only one who wants to confront the toxic person or situation, while everyone else looks the other way, you may feel trapped, powerless, frustrated, or even hopeless. Not to mention that the toxic person who is creating the toxic environment interprets the lack of response of those around him/her as tacit support or "silent affirmation."

It can be exhausting and frustrating.

The skill kit in this book has worked for me countless times. It will work for you. Maybe not all the time (an impossible promise), but the techniques and tools do work. The stories you'll encounter will be proof of this. I love telling stories and that is how I train in my workshop or seminars. You may relate to many of these stories because they're pulled from my life experience, which often resembles your life experience. The stories may make you angry at times, cry at times, or just bust out laughing because you've *been there*.

This book is also part journal. I find my work is like therapy for me. It is helpful to write down your thoughts, reflections and, most importantly, your insights. Your notes may trigger new levels of awareness and learning. So, dive in with me, headfirst! No one is watching. There is just you, this book, and your thoughts.

Like the articles on my website diversitydtg.com, I write for the easily distracted, the million-things-on-your-mind-at-once person. Each section or chapter is short and to the point, and you have to do something. Why? To keep your attention! Put this book on your nightstand with a pen or pencil and just do a couple of pages per night. I hope it grabs you and you finish it right away, but I can also be patient. I will wait for you.

If you want this book to have an even greater possible impact on you, read it with a close friend, partner, or spouse. They might help you be more reflective and you can hold each other accountable when faced with toxic situations in real life. We will be dealing with toxic individuals and toxic environments in all facets of your life: work, home, school, and family. I want to help you on all fronts.

Give this book to that person you know who is just tormenting you with their toxic behavior. You have kept quiet all this time. Give it to them with a signed note inside the cover or give it to them anonymously.

When you are finished reading and interacting with this book, I hope you will ask yourself, "Am I seeing things differently?"

CHAPTER 1.

THE TOXIC PERSON AND THEIR BEHAVIORS

Who do you think of when you hear the word *toxic*? Is it a family member, a bully from school, a work colleague? I suspect one person will pop into your head at first. But I believe you have had multiple run-ins with toxic individuals and situations throughout your life. You might be dealing with a toxic person and their behaviors right now! Maybe that's why you purchased my book.

When confronting a toxic person and their behaviors, how did you react or respond? Did you say or do anything? In my experience, people often suffer in silence. I wrote this book for all the silent sufferers.

Toxic behavior was at the top of my mind when I introduced my soon-to-be wife to meet my immigrant parents, Antonio and Irma. This first encounter was a dumpster fire on a slow-moving train wreck going off a cliff. I knew my parents would not approve. Too many of us know this about our parents, right? I love my parents, and we have had many teachable moments—sometimes they teach me and sometimes I teach them. We should live and learn together, right?

But when I call out toxic behavior with my parents, I often hear: "I didn't mean it the way you took it!"

Do you ever feel like you're parenting your parents?

Here is the big question, the million dollar question (think lawsuit): **How do I get people to understand (especially toxic individuals) that it is the result, the consequence, the impact of their actions that matter and not their intentions?**

A physicist would say, "Every action has a reaction." The perpetrator or the initiator of the behavior is one party, and the target or the receiver of the behavior is the second party. How the receiver or the target experiences or feels is what matters here.

"I did not mean to hurt or offend you" has no bearing after the fact. The comments, the actions have "landed" on the target or object of said behaviors. Now buckle up—here's how the evening played out between my parents and my future wife. Recognize any of these moments within your experience?

"DEAD ON ARRIVAL"

I fell in love with Kelly Elizabeth and I knew she was the one, so I had to bring her home. I called ahead to grease the skids, trying to head off some of the toxicity at the pass. Being proactive and anticipating toxic behaviors can be helpful!

My mom's first two questions were: "What is her name and where is she from?"

I pretend like I don't hear her and I jump ahead. My parents are immigrants from Colombia, South America, and I am bringing home a White Southern Belle with an accent that blew me away, green eyes, and perfect teeth—not the Latina they are hoping for.

"*Mamá, cuando visitemos, quiero la sala, el cristal, los platos de su boda, etc.*"

"Mama, when we visit, I want the living room, the crystal, the china from your wedding. I want the best—roll out the red carpet."

I am implying to my mother that Kelly is the one.

"This is exciting," my mother replies. "What is her name and where is she from?" Mom repeats the unanswered question.

I ignore the question again. "See you Thursday," I say and end the call.

We pull into the driveway of my childhood home. As we are getting out of the car, I see my mom in the front kitchen window (exactly where I expect her to be). I wave. She does not wave back—she looks disappointed. She puts her hand over her brow and shakes her head from side to side.

Kelly looks at me, sees my expression of concern, and asks, "What's wrong?"

"You're dead on arrival," I answer.

"Wait, what? I'm wearing my best!"

"Kelly, we have to go to Plan B."

"Plan B?" she asks with a curious look on her face. "What was Plan A?"

I hurry to explain. "Plan A is they would like you for who you are and, well, they clearly already have issues with who you are not. Come with me to the trunk of the car for Plan B." I open the trunk and pull out two packages.

"What are we looking at?" Kelly asks.

"Gifts. In my culture you bring gifts."

"I'm not from your culture," Kelly interjects.

"Exactly. That is why these gifts are extra big. I purchased these gifts for you to give to my parents, but don't tell them I purchased them; I want them to think you brought the gifts! This will be our first lie, an error of omission."

I don't give Kelly time to react because we are at the front door.

My mom opens the door and she looks great in her Easter best. Velvet red top, black velvet pants, patent leather belt and matching shoes, every piece of expensive jewelry attached to her face and body. My mom looks like an expensive impulse tower at Macy's. Kelly glances at me for guidance as she offers my mom her gift.

My mom says, "Oh, Kelly, you should not have brought me a gift—and my favorite as well."

My mom gives Kelly a big hug, and Kelly looks at me with this face: "I can't breathe." I smile like: "Welcome to our culture. Got to love the lack of personal space, hugs, and kisses right on the cheek." Kelly looks smothered.

Then my father, Antonio, steps out from behind my mom in a V-neck T-shirt, cutoff sleeves, what looks like "hand torn" denim shorts, rope for a belt, and sandals (*chanclas* made from run-down tires for the sole of the shoe and leather straps). My father's appearance, meant to intimidate, is a bad omen for our first meeting. Kelly looks startled, but nevertheless she hands my father his gift and he gives her a bear hug. The early conversation goes well, then Kelly excuses herself to the bathroom.

"How could you?" my mother erupts as soon as Kelly is out of sight. "Is she Catholic? Is she one of us? Can she cook? Where is this Lynchburg, Virginia?"

"Will she bear fruit?" my father asks. "Does she keep a clean house?"

"Bear fruit?" I repeat.

Toxic people point out all the negative, all the differences between them and us, right?

When Kelly returns, she squeezes back onto the love seat beside me. My mother turns to my father.

"*A mí no me gusta,*" says my mother. *I don't like her.*

"*A mí tampoco,*" replies my father. *Me neither.*

They didn't know that Kelly could speak Spanish. I squeeze her hand, suggesting without words *don't say anything, don't let them know you speak Spanish*. The torturous evening continues with a barrage of questions. What is the one question they never ask because they are emotionally hijacked by their toxic biases?

Do you love her? The subject never comes up.

As we are getting our coats and leaving, I whisper in my mother's ear in Spanish. *Kelly habla Espanol.* Kelly speaks Spanish. Kelly is already out at the car.

My mom is stunned. "What? Oh, please tell her we didn't mean all those things we said about her. Oh, this is what I get for having a diversity trainer as a son."

"What? Don't blame me, Mama. Your actions have consequences, and what you meant has no bearing here. Not to mention you moved our family to an all-white neighborhood when I was single digits—and you are surprised I did not fall in love with a Latina? I have grown up in a predominately white neighborhood, culture, and environment."

My parents were surprised I wanted to marry Kelly, and of course they wanted me to marry a Latina. I pointed out many times: "You moved to McLean, Virginia, and there were 'very few Latinos' in McLean." Back then, "mixed marriages" were rare. Curious, I did a little research.

According to the Pew Research Center, "One-in-six newlyweds are married to someone of a different race or ethnicity." Pew goes on to point out in their report *Intermarriage in the US 50 years After Loving v. Virginia*, in 2015, 17 percent of all US newlyweds had a spouse of a different race or ethnicity, marking more than a fivefold increase since 1967, when 3 percent of newlyweds were intermarried, according to a new Pew Research Center analysis of US Census Bureau data. In that year, the US Supreme Court in the *Loving v. Virginia* case ruled that marriage across racial lines was legal throughout the country. Until this ruling, interracial marriages were forbidden in many states.[1]

INTENT VERSUS IMPACT

Have you been in a similar situation as Kelly and me?

Again, I love my parents, but their behavior can be toxic. To understand why you may hear "stop being so sensitive" when you try to stand up for yourself and others against toxic behaviors, we need to understand your intent versus the impact of your actions (consequences). I'm going to show you why impact is what's most important, not intent. Remember, the old adage "It's the thought that counts" implies you know their thought(s). We can't read each other's mind; we have to rely on what we see, their comments, their actions, their body language. Way too many people try to excuse their toxic behaviors by saying, "I did not mean it or I intended something different or you are taking it the wrong way." Again, I can't read your mind. All I have to go on is what I see, feel, and understand.

You hear this all the time (especially in an election year): "Freedom of Speech" and I always add "And with this freedom comes the consequence of your speech. Yes, you can say whatever you want, but there are always consequences." I think many people want to have the freedom to speak and then don't take into consideration the consequences, don't want to be held accountable for the consequences of their speech. Not how it works.

I conducted interviews as background research for this book. My interviews showed people are conflict avoiders (most at work and at home) and/or don't know how to address the toxic behaviors in their workplaces and families. Employers provide very little to no training—it is an ambush, a setup. No training provided for family conflict or drama either, right? Here's the training I wish people received.

WE DON'T KNOW THE INTENTIONS OF OTHERS

We all mean well. I never question the intent behind any person's actions. We actually don't know the intentions of the other person, but we assume their intentions based on the behavior we see, how we react (our feelings), or the kind of relationship we have with the perpetrator. This is the first mistake. We should look at the behavior(s) in question and only the behavior(s).

The Anti-Defamation League has some great resources on unpacking and understanding this tension: the difference between the intent of our actions versus the actual consequences of our actions. ADL's "Intent vs. Impact: Why Does it Matter"[2] and "When it Comes to

Bias, We Must Prioritize Impact Over Intent" articles and related lesson plans for students, teachers, and parents are fabulous resources—especially if you are a parent.[3]

WHAT MATTERS IS WHAT YOU SAID, NOT WHAT YOU MEANT

I find too many people will get defensive when the target confronts the perpetrator about the behavior(s). The perpetrator typically responds with: "I didn't mean it the way you took it." Often, in my travels, people don't want to be held accountable for their actions. Unfortunately, this does not take the sting out of the behavior(s).

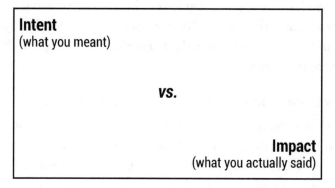

What matters is what you said, not what you meant.

I see this a lot with family interactions: "I didn't mean that" or "Stop being so sensitive." Now we call that "blaming the victim or target." Don't forget the perpetrator (the toxic person) has no problem telling you how to feel. We should all try to understand how the other person came to feel the way they feel; but to tell people how to feel is a common trait of a toxic person. You must own your own emotions!

THE REASONABLE PERSON STANDARD

I often employ a standard from my sexual harassment prevention work: it is called the *Reasonable Person Standard*. Would a reasonable person in said workplace expect to see or experience toxic behaviors? Of course not. Think of your family. Would a reasonable member of your family expect to be treated with respect and dignity and love or rather be treated disrespectfully, hatefully, and in a toxic manner? Should kids in school reasonably expect to be bullied and teased or treated with respect and dignity? Civility, dignity, respect for all is the standard for all, period.

The Reasonable Person Standard can be traced back to the 1837 case Vaughan v. Menlove in the English courts. This standard helps us remain objective about the expectations and behaviors in a workplace, school, or family, rather than subjective.[4]

I have asked my parents many times, "What are you doing, what are you saying?" They reply with, "Oh, I did not mean it" or "I don't understand how or why you took it that way!" Then I poll the rest of the family: "Am I the only one concerned or offended here? How would you have received that comment?"

I share the polling results with my parents. They might try to discount the poll results by saying, "Oh, Mauricio, you are just influencing everybody." But they eventually come to grips with the consequences of their actions. I hold them accountable, and I recruit others in my family to do the same. Sometimes it is what they don't know they don't know, and they try to hide behind intent instead of focusing on the impact of their actions on others. If they don't own the consequences of their actions, I tell them there will be "consequences to you not owning your consequences."

OWN THE IMPACT OF YOUR ACTIONS

If you find yourself being called out for toxic behavior, don't take it personally. Apologize for your comment or behavior. Don't try to avoid your responsibility. Step up to the plate. Don't focus on your intentions because no one knew your intentions. Try to put yourself in the target's shoes and understand their feelings. Put your feelings aside. This is not about you—the perpetrator—this is about the target. Try to empathize with the target and focus on the impact of your actions.

Apologize and ask the target to always come and share their feelings whenever they feel wronged. I know some of you are not comfortable when someone else shows or shares their feelings. Become approachable. Try to understand this discomfort. I am comfortable as the author of this book in helping you engage your discomfort. One of the hardest things to do is to become comfortable being uncomfortable. This space is where learning and personal growth truly happens.

You want to be perceived as humble, approachable, and you are open to learning from any one incident. You don't want to be seen as rigid or inflexible. I often hear, "I am an old dog and you can't teach an old dog new tricks!" I always respond with, "Well, we can get you a kennel somewhere else!" Meaning they are going to get fired. What you don't want to do is seem defensive or stubborn. Reach out! This is a wake-up call that you need to improve this relationship.

I often come across toxic individuals who do not want to own their actions and the consequences of their actions.

They don't want to apologize or don't like apologizing, period. They see apologizing as a sign of weakness. The higher you climb in an organization, the better you must become at understanding this simple truth. Be humble, own your actions and their consequences, and apologize.

SEPARATE THE PERSON FROM THEIR BEHAVIORS

This book is dedicated to separating the toxic behaviors from the person. I use the phrase "Toxic Individual or Person or In-Law" to get your attention, but really, we must separate the person from their toxic behaviors and focus on their actions and the impact these have on the people subjected to these behaviors.

If you attack the person (and not their behaviors), they will get defensive, dig in their heels, and never listen. The conflict is likely to get worse. Don't react to the behaviors. You can see every day in the media situations where emotions got the best of the parties involved. My parents were emotionally hijacked, and I just did not want to get caught up in their emotional biases.

I just stayed calm, cool, and collected and did not get angry or show anger toward my parents. I love my parents, and I can separate them from their emotions and actions. I have pointed out to them many times how "that first night was really embarrassing for me." I don't know what their intent was, but they embarrassed themselves and me in the process.

Journal: Can you think of examples in your own life when your actions did not really reflect your intent behind them? List some examples. Be specific, include all details.

CHAPTER 2.

HOW UNAWARE ARE YOU? NARCISSISM AT ITS BEST!

"You can't talk yourself out of what you behaved your way into. You have to behave your way out."

—STEPHEN COVEY

Too often in my career, I have come across the naive, the ignorant "bad actor" who claims not to know, not to understand—they claim to be unaware of how their actions affect others. I often wonder if they are playing coy and actually know but do not care. However, their employer cares, and since nobody has said anything up until this point, I am hired to come in and investigate and give the "tough love," the feedback no one else has the courage or the skill to give and to hold this person accountable for their actions and the consequences of their actions.

HE CLAIMS TO NOT KNOW HE IS A SEXIST

A client hired me to give their CEO some feedback.

"What am I looking for?" I asked.

"You'll know when you see it," replied their Human Resources representative. "We don't want to bias you in any way."

The CEO was in a few meetings back-to-back and I was asked to watch him run meetings and then give him some feedback. I, of course, recorded the meetings in case the CEO wanted to deny he did not say this or that.

After the two meetings, the CEO sits down with me and asks, "What is all of this about?"

"You have no idea why your company hired me to give you some feedback?" I ask.

"No, not really."

"First, I am not the only one concerned here. I am not the only who notices your actions and their consequences. You are not reading the room. Your colleagues at the Executive Level, watch them—their facial expressions, their looks of surprise, some with almost embarrassingly painful looks and half smiles, almost nervous."

"What are you talking about?"

"You constantly interrupt and cut off the women on your team when they are saying something, trying to make a point, laying out a solution to a particular problem. You often raise your voice a little, cut her off, and worse, you try to finish her statement for her because you think you know where she is going. You were wrong nearly every time as the woman in particular corrected you with 'no, that is not where I was going.' Is this about trying to save time? Because you made the meetings run longer instead with your interruptions. Now with the men on your team, you let them finish their points. You seem much more patient with them."

"I had no idea."

"Really? I can play back some of the video if you'd like."

"No, no, I have to think about this, what I am doing here, I had no idea."

"No one has ever told you that you are sexist?" (Just tell it like it is; it's what I am paid for.)

"Who complained? Was it the women on my team?"

"What? And make a career-ending complaint that balloons into an uncomfortable situation? No, you seem to do this all the time, in other meetings with lower-level personnel in the room or on the call. More witnesses than we can all count. No, it was the men on your team who just can't take it anymore. I think they are actually embarrassed for you."

"I think the women on my team can be overly sensitive."

I am stunned at his reaction. Now, I get a bit more animated.

"Listen, it is one thing to be unaware, or in denial, but then to blame the women for your blind spot? Come on. You can't tell other people how to feel. This is the trifecta of toxicity. You have to own your actions and the consequences of those actions, and you cannot blame the victims of your toxicity, or rather abrogate your responsibility for your actions. Your sexism is obvious to all in your meetings, and the fact that you are the last to know—really unbelievable."

"So, what do I do now?"

"Well, I recommend you apologize to your whole team: I mean show real contrition. Not like you are faking it or going through the motions. You have to be sincere, genuine. Hide behind me: you received some feedback from an executive coach. Then I would apologize to each person individually, privately, and even throw in a note afterward, handwritten, personal."

What troubles me here and all too often is the men never say anything in the meeting. They are bystanders. Too many people just watching and saying nothing. This CEO could interpret their silence as tacit support: they are okay with how their CEO is running their meetings when really, they are exhausted. Why? Because the CEO is their boss? Are they intimidated by him and his power? Do they really need to hire me? I mean, these guys could just say something. "Ouch" or "really" or something related. The women are tired of this treatment, and their male colleagues not coming to their aid only exacerbates the situation. Is this power dynamics or fear or both? *This CEO seems nice, but he is intimidating*, I think.

One of the most common questions I get is how to stand up for yourself or others in the moment.

WHO'S UP NEXT?

I sit on a couch outside a ballroom in upstate New York, and I'm waiting to speak to several hundred partners of a major national labor and employment law firm. These workshops are tricky because attorneys (not all of them, but many) can be argumentative, difficult, and challenge me and my presentation, especially because I am not an attorney. With a newspaper hiding my face, I eavesdrop on the two gatekeepers at the door.

"Who's up next?" one of the lawyers asks.

"Some bullshit presentation on diversity and inclusion," the other attorney scoffs.

This a Labor and Employment law firm! I think.

The head of the firm opens the door, sticks his head out, and spots me. "Mauricio," he says, "you're up!"

As I walk in, I look at both partners right in their eyes. "I am that bullshit diversity trainer," I say. "Excuse me."

They both shrink and say nothing as I pass them and head up to the stage where I take my spot.

I roast the two gatekeepers using that "Toxic Moment of Truth" as a gift to start my presentation. I do not embarrass them specifically, protecting their identities, but I burn them in front of everybody. I'm well-practiced at this. I experience these moments often. After being called out like this, they both sit dutifully through my workshop. At the session's end, they approach me.

"You are really good," one of the attorneys said. "You made us look like fools."

I laughed. "Well, you said it."

This was a small moment of toxic behavior that only involved three people. Some levels of toxicity have higher stakes and can involve entire organizations—with serious consequences.

You never know who is listening? The "walls have eyes and ears" is another way of telling this story. I find toxic individuals and their toxic behaviors can come across as reckless, insensitive. This cavalier, "I don't care who is listening" attitude is amusing to me because you never know who is listening. Are your comments really going unnoticed or do you have an opportunity to hold them to account?

So many of the interviews I conduct reflect individuals with stories of callous, almost reckless toxic people and their behaviors, and although maybe the toxic individuals do not care who they hurt, they definitely care when unintended consequences undermine their credibility or derail their career. "Hot shots" my father called them—hot shots until someone throws ice cold water on them.

I'M NOT INTERESTED IN BLACK LIVES MATTER

So much of my work is driven by current events. A real moment of truth for my field, a flash point, was 9/11. Everything used to be "before or after 9/11." More recently, the whole George Floyd tragedy stirred up a lot of emotions, issues, potential for toxicity—an opportunity for some to just be outright insensitive.

A client calls me to describe a recent town hall meeting (virtual). Their CEO is going over the most recent numbers. Everything is scripted, but he chooses to end the town hall with an off-the-cuff remark.

"Oh, and one more thing," he says. "I am getting a lot of inquiries about 'what is our position, what are we going to do about George Floyd, the whole Black Lives Matter situation.' Let me be very clear by saying I don't want to get involved in this political firestorm. I don't care about BLM." Then, he ends the call. First bomb goes off. Rank and file go berserk.

Soon after, the VP of human resources rushes into the CEO's office. "I can't believe you ended the town hall that way," she says. "Black Lives Matter is very important to many of our employees."

"What do you care?" he replies. "You're a White woman!"

She tells me she kept her cool. "Look, I am not just talking about our African American or Black employees here. There are many advocates, allies, and people who really empathize with the plight of the African American people in this country." He ignored her plea. This VP was a very well-respected member of the senior management team, and many employees valued her for her moral and ethical standards; she was a trusted senior leader.

Soon, the organization was in full crisis mode. Emails and voicemails swamped human resources. Board members received a firehose of emails and calls. It was all over social media. Eventually, they called me in to work with the CEO. The first thing out of his mouth was: "Why is everyone so bent out of shape over what I said? I was clear. I do not want to get involved. I think people are making a mountain out of a mole hill."

He was upset that people were upset. Figure that out.

"Look," I said, leveling with him. "What your employees heard was someone who does not care. You'd made up your mind without any discussion. You decided that the topic of George Floyd is too political, and you don't care. You don't see the humanity of it all."

"Well, I don't."

He begrudgingly sent out a video apology. What I mean is: his apology did not come across as sincere or heartfelt. People could tell. His employees commented to each other "that it appeared he had his arm twisted behind his back to put out a short video and a statement." His reputation was forever harmed, and his efficacy as a leader would never be the same. People can have long memories.

I might add, I think this apology, this mea culpa needed to *not be* a short video and note. Let your employees see your remorse, your concern. Show vulnerability.

Some clients don't listen to me. Also, why I think people just didn't believe him, did not buy his story: it was a very short video and a short note. A short statement? I mean really fall on your sword, explain in detail what you were thinking and accompany it with a heartfelt longer note.

This CEO had no idea what the reaction to his comments would be or, worse, he didn't care. He wanted all to know where he stood on the issues without considering what his rank and file felt about the issues. He was caught off guard. I was like "Really." He lacks emotional intelligence. He didn't understand how his comments, his emotional state, triggered his devastating comments that would land on his employee population in a very incendiary and insensitive manner. I would suggest meeting with some employees, many really, and ask them to explain how he and his comments made them feel. Listen first, get many perspectives, and then follow up with a heartfelt video-based apology and a longer note acknowledging he listened to rank and file. Listening first, enlisting input and feedback, encouraging it, did not happen.

Yes, he is potentially a narcissist (an ongoing theme in this book) with an incredible ego. Does he know this or admit to this? I'm not sure, but clearly all this contributed to him begrudgingly and without sincerity giving an apology.

ACTIVE DISENGAGEMENT

This CEO's behavior is an example of *active disengagement*. These are the folks I consider toxic, known for saying and doing toxic things regularly that can upset people. They like to disrupt, almost being provocative to shock. This can be the ROJ—Retired on the Job—with an attitude. The RIP—Retired in Place—with a purpose to poison everyone around them. This cannot be your CEO.

You see, if you are quiet, just doing your job, no one knows you are unhappy or, better, you are not sharing or trying to spread your unhappiness, I am okay with you. However, it is the person who is actively disengaged—spreading rumor, being negative, looking for fault in everything—who is truly the problem here. Now typically, we see this person coming. Again, these toxic behaviors and actions build.

"You are the CEO," I said to this guy. "You're not just talking like you are some average employee of the company. You don't have that luxury. Some work here out of respect for you, what you represent, your guidance, your vision, your values, what you stand for. You can choose to make said comments, but you can't choose the consequences of those comments. Digging in, being indignant, and choosing not to apologize will only throw gasoline on this fire.

"You must apologize immediately. The shock waves of your comments are shaking the company to its core. It is all over social media, your board is concerned, and employees are quitting, en masse."

This CEO eventually came around and apologized, but it did not come across as authentic, heartfelt, or genuine. I was told his video apology was then followed by something in writing but, again, it did not land well. Both were too short and not authentic. Being authentic is hard for some people.

THE TOWER OF TOXICITY

Not all active disengagement is the same. There are degrees of toxicity. I would like to introduce you to the "Tower of Toxicity."

Level I—*Toxic Candidate*—At the bottom of the tower is the person who is quiet, checked out, not participating, but by looking at their body language you surmise something is wrong. This is a red flag!

You know that much (80 percent or more) of what we are thinking we communicate nonverbally. You can tell how I feel just by looking at me. This person does not help, does not participate, does not go the extra mile. If we don't talk to this candidate because of their toxicity, don't inquire, don't show we care, they might get worse, for toxicity escalates. *Are you okay? Everything all right?*

You want to "engage the disengaged" as quickly as possible. Let the toxic person know that "we know something is up." I tend to be more up-front: *You okay,* really?

Level II—*Toxic Starter*—This is the toxic person who is unhappy; everyone but the manager or teacher or parent or preacher knows it. They are constantly spreading their negative views and opinions when the supervisor or the manager or the teacher or the parent is not present. Again, they are passive around superiors, but when superiors are not present, they light up like a bonfire.

In the previous story with the two "gatekeeper" lawyers at the labor and employment workshop, the toxic attorneys were exhibiting Level II behavior.

Eventually, someone will go to the "higher authority" because they just cannot take it anymore. Often called passive-aggressive, we know who these folks are! Because people eventually stop listening to the toxic person.

Level III—*Toxic Manipulator*—is when the toxic person is toxic even in front of the supervisor or manager, almost daring the higher authority to respond. By the time the toxic person is at Level III, they are emboldened, difficult, and energized, and it is more challenging to "wrestle them to a place of reason." You see, we all have to learn to respond to toxicity and not react.

Any exhibition of these toxic behaviors can have detrimental effects to an organization and those an organization serves. By the time I'm called in to personally coach an executive, the person is already exhibiting Level III behavior.

The through line, the theme with all three of these stories is narcissism. I was a psychology and economics double major in college at the University of Virginia, and I really like the take on narcissism at psychologytoday.com. According to Psychology Today, narcissism is characterized by a grandiose sense of self-importance, a lack of empathy for others, a need for excessive admiration, and the belief that one is unique and deserving of special treatment.[1] Sound like anyone you know?

SKILL/TOOL—"OUCH"

The first line of defense against toxic behaviors is to know when to say something and how to say it.

You are calm, cool, and collected. You are being rational; you are coming from the rational side of your brain. A horrible comment is made (no one else has said anything yet, now or before). Now the person exhibiting the toxic behavior has to be informed that they have crossed a respectful, civil line. Who draws the line? Well, each of us has a line of decency, of civility. We all have boundaries, right? I guess the problem is that for some of us they are blurred, or we are not willing (fear) to tell people when they have crossed a line of respect, civility, decency.

But I am talking here about a toxic comment that is universally not appropriate, respectful, or civil outside the bounds of professional discourse or civil family interactions. Again, any "reasonable person" would find such conduct unwelcome, uncomfortable, and really not relevant to their work and workplace.

Let's start simple, easy. The toxic behavior, say the n-word, or c##t, or f####t, b###h, or some other objectively offensive word or statement is uttered. **All blanks are a bunch of blanks** (you can fill in the rest). Now you have heard this person say it before, or maybe this is the first time, and you want the person to know you are not okay with this comment or phrase (they crossed the line). I recommend starting with this myriad of responses. Also, you notice (you are reading the room) that you are not the only one uncomfortable with the toxic word or phrase or pattern of toxic behaviors.

Responses to toxic behaviors:
- "Ouch." (my favorite)
- "Excuse me?"
- "No, no. Not here, not now."
- "Wow."
- "Really?"
- "Hey now" or "Come on now"..."we are all family." (at home)
- "You are going to say that here and now?"
- "Come on, you are going to say that, here, now at work/home?"
- "How is your comment work-related?" (take the high ground)
- "Do you think your comment is 'family respectful or family friendly'?"
- "Unbelievable." (when the comment is really bad)
- "Are you okay?" (one of my favorites: conveys concern that they might not be in their right mind or something else is going on)

Repeating what they said immediately after they said it is also powerful.

Of course, in a group if the person who uses toxic language is being called out by more than one person using the above language, they will at least pause, maybe think twice before continuing the toxic banter. Groups of people (bystanders) who all or most speak up at the same time (upstanders) hold power. Imagine the positive "group vibe or peer pressure."

In each of the "moments of truth" toxic situations in this chapter, if people around the toxic behavior launcher had said "ouch" or "come on" or "hey now," maybe, just maybe, this toxic person would at least pause for a moment to think about what they are saying and doing and, more important, how their actions are being received and felt by others.

Journalize: Have you seen this before? Been in the room? Did anybody say anything? Seen this before?

THE RESEARCH IS QUITE CLEAR

I dove into writing this book based on my professional work experience to date assessing, coaching, and training over one million participants with hundreds of clients in my nearly thirty-year career. Upon the recommendation of my editor, I started to do some research as well as conduct some interviews to verify my premises about toxicity and toxic behaviors in the workplace (and at home). My premises and beliefs were confirmed.

MIT Sloan School of Management Senior Lecturer Donald Sull and a cofounder of CultureX, Charles Sull, cofounder of CultureX, and Ben Zweig, CEO of Revelio Labs and an adjunct professor of economics at NYU Stern School of Business put out some fascinating research in January of 2022. Clearly COVID has pushed organizations to their limit. My premise was toxic workplaces and toxic managers were at the center of the Great Resignation. My instincts were spot-on!

In their report "Toxic Culture is Driving the Great Resignation," these authors said, "More than 40 percent of all employees were thinking about leaving their jobs at the beginning of 2021, and as the year went on, workers quit in unprecedented numbers. Between April and September 2021, more than 24 million American employees left their jobs, an all-time record. As the Great Resignation rolls on, business leaders are struggling to make sense of the factors driving the mass exodus. More importantly, they are looking for ways to hold on to valued employees."[2]

To better understand the sources of the Great Resignation and help leaders respond effectively, they analyzed thirty-four million online employee profiles to identify US workers who left their employer for any reason (including quitting, retiring, or being laid off) between April and September 2021. "The data, from Revelio Labs, where one of us (Ben) is the CEO, enabled us to estimate company-level attrition rates for the Culture 500, a sample of large, mainly for-profit companies that together employ nearly one-quarter of the private-sector workforce in the United States."[3]

They go on to say in their comprehensive report, "we found that corporate culture is more important than burnout or compensation in predicting which companies lost employees at a higher rate than their industries as a whole. A toxic corporate culture is the single best predictor of which companies suffered from high attrition in the first six months of the Great Resignation."[4]

TOP PREDICTORS OF ATTRITION DURING THE GREAT RESIGNATION

The authors analyzed the impact of more than 170 cultural topics on employee attrition in Culture 500 companies from April through September 2021. These five topics were the leading predictors of attrition. Each score indicates the level of importance of each topic for attrition relative to employee compensation. A toxic culture is 10.4 times more likely to contribute to attrition than compensation.[5]

Toxic corporate culture: **10.4 times**
Job insecurity and reorganization: **3.5 times**
High levels of innovation: **3.2 times**
Failure to recognize employee performance: **2.9 times**
Poor response to COVID-19: **1.8 times**

I conducted dozens of interviews with people across many sectors from professional sports to healthcare to engineering and technology firms. The interviews were clear: the toxic individuals and their behaviors are often ignored because the toxic person is seen as successful, important, competent, and skilled technically, and we accept this toxic bad with good.

They have no interpersonal skills, no human relations skills, and they are just accepted as "so and so is just that way." No one gives them feedback or holds them accountable, and this normalization or acceptance allows the toxic person room to roam. They are given latitude "to just be themselves" as long as they get results. Saying something like "Ouch" is the first step to alerting the toxic person to their toxic behaviors and their impact on the workplace.

Journal: Do you have a narcissist in your life? How do you respond (not react)?

CHAPTER 3.

ANGER MANAGEMENT— KNOW YOUR TRIGGERS

Anger begets anger and can spin out of control. Have you ever gotten so angry you lost control? Have you ever experienced being the object of someone's wrath? Have you ever gotten so angry you forgot what happened, what originally triggered your rage? Sometimes we are observers of life, like it is happening to us, but we just watch. Sometimes we are more active or more present, and maybe this comes with maturity and experience. In this chapter, we start to talk about "getting involved," that is, being more active. From bystander to upstander. Whether the toxic behaviors are directed at you or you are just present, this book is about "getting in the game" and "getting off the sidelines."

"MY FATHER'S RAGE!" PART 1

I was sixteen when I said to my father, casually, in front of my mom, "I think you're being cheap here, Papa!"

Remember, my father was an immigrant from Colombia. He immigrated here (legally), learned English, served in the military, and didn't get his college degree until after serving, through the GI Bill. He was thirty-two years old when he graduated from Queens College, Queens, New York.

He punched me right in the face. I fell to the ground. I could not feel my feet. Did I still have my shoes on?

My mom erupted with tears and screamed at my dad "to not get so angry!" She knew my father's rage.

"I will never forget what you just did! You hit me in the face, hard!" I said to my father.

My father stormed off. He never apologized, by the way. To the day my father passed, he never said "I love you," or "I'm sorry," or "I'm proud of you!" And please don't tell me, "That is their generation." What a cop-out. I say it all the time to my wife and kids: "I love you, I am proud of you." They hear it from me more in a week than I ever heard it my whole life.

For my father, anything to do with money and being frugal (cheap) was taboo. A trigger, so to speak. I learned this the hard way.

We all learn from our quick-to-temper parents. You better watch out for the telltale signs of anger approaching: don't escalate, don't fuel the coming rage. Be ready to walk away. Let things cool down. Also "understand your battles." What contributing factors were present? Something else was going on. For context, my parents were possibly having financial or money issues.

I stepped right into that minefield, frankly ill-prepared for the consequences. In this story, I just watched this dumpster fire on a slow-moving train wreck going off a cliff. I was young and inexperienced. I was truly naive on how to deal with such matters. It was also cultural. My father was the "boss, our fearless family leader." You did not talk back to him; you did not disrespect him.

"KNOW YOUR TRIGGERS."

I coach executives. I train workshop participants every day to learn the difference between reacting (being hijacked by your own emotions) and responding (cool head prevails) to a particular behavior or set of behaviors. Responding comes from reason, common sense, and the rational part of your brain. Unfortunately, before we can respond, we must first learn not to react.

According to Daniel Kahneman, there are two parts to our brain: the "System 1" or fast-thinking part of your brain and "System 2," or slow-thinking, rational part of your brain.[1] When we experience something, the stimuli run up the cerebral cortex to the fast thinking part of the brain where emotions rule. Don't let your emotions hijack you: stay present, take deep breaths, give yourself some time, pause. Are you present in the moment? Wait until the slow thinking or commonsensical, rational part of your brain can take over. Stay calm, cool, and collected; pause, and the slow or rational part of your brain will take control. This is why mindfulness is such a hot emerging field today. With technology all around us distracting us from being present, being mindful and in the moment is one of the hardest things to do every moment of the day.

In other words, whenever we are subject to stimuli—comments, behaviors, actions—the stimuli are interpreted and processed first in the emotional part of your brain. If you learn to not react from the emotional part of your brain and to wait instead, to give yourself a little time (a couple of minutes) and then respond, you will ensure that you are not emotionally hijacked by your own triggers. Triggers are particular behaviors or actions that just get your goat, that jack you up from zero to sixty in seconds. Often our parents can trigger us rather easily.

I know this has happened to you. Have you ever received an email or a text that just got you fired up? You quickly replied with an angry, passionate email or text. Minutes later you were like, "Oh, I should not have sent that." That was the emotional part of your brain hijacking you and later the rational part of your brain second guessing, reminding you that you could respond in a much better, more reasonable way versus an emotional reaction.

Know your triggers. What sets you off? Think of all of the times you lost control, you got really angry, and then later you were frustrated with yourself for losing control. Do an inventory, and the next time one of these triggers manifests itself, know to walk away, take a break, and get control of yourself.

Typically, I might write the angry text or email and leave it there, without sending it. Then I would walk away, maybe ask a colleague to read it. Just create an excuse, a task: go to the bathroom, get a cup of coffee, go check the mail, go get lunch, and before I even get back to my desk, I know not to send that email or text.

Remember, in most toxic moments of truth when you are facing horrible behavior, you have a choice to react immediately or to take a moment to allow for reflection; let the commonsensical,rational part of your brain come up with a response.

I have these three questions posted in my office:
1. Does this situation need or demand a response?
2. Does this situation need or demand a response from me?
3. Does this situation need or demand a response from me right now?

Just asking yourself these three questions calmly can move you from the reactionary, emotional knee-jerk response mode to the more commonsensical, rational response mode or part of your brain.

"MY FATHER'S RAGE!" PART 2

Flash forward to my son Ethan saying exactly the same thing (he was also sixteen) to me that I said to my father a generation earlier. We were out in the front yard on a gorgeous day having a conversation, and Ethan said, "I think you are being cheap, Dad!" I immediately felt my heart racing and my hackles "rage up"—I went from zero to anger—rage—in seconds. Oh, my goodness. I had a flashback immediately to when I was sixteen talking to my father.

I looked at Ethan. "Wow, I said the exact same thing to Abuelo (his grandfather) when I was your age!"

Like my father, my forehead gives me away, and Ethan senses I am getting hot. My father had this vein in his forehead that would just pop. I, too, wear my anger on my brow.

"What happened?" Ethan asked.

"He punched me right in the face, and I fell to the ground."

I had thought my father had broken my nose. I wanted to punch Ethan (I am my father's son with a similar proclivity to anger), but instead I turned away. Every part of my soul, my being, wanted to hurt Ethan, to inflict hurt and pain. But instead, I turned away. I could feel my anger welling up.

I am self-aware and emotionally intelligent enough to know that I could not let my anger get the better of me as it often did my father. Funny thing though—an idea flashed into my head briefly: "Call Papa." I was ready to call my father on my mobile phone and ask, *Papa, can you come over and bring the old belt with the rusty buckle? I need a pinch hitter here to finish off my son.* For a second, I thought about it, then paused, then laughed at myself—that nervous kind of laugh, part remembering back and part *don't do it.*

Ethan came up behind me, hugged me, and said, "I'm sorry."

"All good," I replied. "I will not let the fear, the violence be passed down to the next generation." As we both were tearing up, all I kept saying to myself was, *No, I will not act out like my father.*

Don't get me wrong—I love my father and miss him dearly, but there are times when I will do exactly what my dad would do, and sometimes I must do the opposite. We all come to that path in the road every day, many times per day. I realized that we can learn from past experiences, from history: do better, or repeat it.

Journalize: Have you been here? How did you respond or react to your similar situation?

"WELL, HE IS BLACK; HE IS GUILTY OF SOMETHING!"

Three couples go out to dinner together: my wife and I with four of our dearest friends. We are talking about current events as we always do, and a particular developing Georgia tragedy comes up. A story was circulating that this one person on death row might actually be innocent. He was going to be put to death soon, and there were appeals that the governor was considering.

I was arguing that all evidence must be considered, especially new evidence when one of the other guys in our group comments: "Well I mean, come on, he is Black; he is guilty of something."

Now I want to jump across the table and punch his lights out (but I know violence is not the answer), and I cannot let my emotions get the best of me. I know not to let myself be emotionally hijacked by own emotions. Now my engine is revving at high RPMs.

Kelly pinches my knee under the table like *don't say anything*. I wait. Nothing. No one says anything. Minutes pass and I am just in shock, amazed that everyone else will let that comment go. Minutes feel like hours. I cannot take this anymore; these are my friends?

I know myself: I can get hot fast (like my father) but also the triggering topic is relevant. We are talking about a person's life hanging in the balance, and he might be innocent. Kelly picks up on it as well. So important to be around people who know you, understand you, and can help you weather the trials and tribulations of such conflict.

I finally say, "No one here is offended by that comment? No one is concerned about that horrible, racist, just *wrong* comment? Wow, you are my friends. This is who I choose to hang out with?"

Shame can be a powerful dynamic, but unfortunately this person has none. He will say things to shock the people listening to him, giggle at himself, then move on in the conversation: very immature if you ask me. He is a jerk.

Finally, his wife chimes in. "Yeah that was horrible and racist." Another person tries to take the other side. "Oh, we know it was just a joke; he was kidding."

I pointed out we don't know the intent of the comment and assuming it was meant to be humorous adds no value.

"No, no, no, unacceptable, this kind of toxic humor is reprehensible, offensive, and cannot be tolerated by anyone, let alone my friends," I said. Needless to say, the tone and tenor of the dinner changed that night, and I went on to no longer hang out with these folks, and I am okay with that. The cavalier nature of these destructive comments was just too much for me. Oh, and to be called "too sensitive" is just adding insult to injury.

Surround yourself with decent, positive, uplifting, inspiring people, and you will live a longer life, I promise.

Journalize: What did you say the last time you were present and an awful, racist, sexist, homophobic, or related hateful comment was uttered in a group? Did you say something? Did you walk away?

Sometimes the situation calls for a third party, a cool head, to prevail, someone with no skin in the game to step in. Someone who is willing to say something (that others are thinking) when no one else will; I am that person. I sometimes just cannot help myself. I have to help; I have to say something. I am a third party, a bystander, but at times a third party can really make a difference, and if I say nothing later, I reflect back: "I should have said something!" I am just upset with myself. Better I speak up at the time than later regret having done nothing. I don't like living a life of regret.

The running theme throughout these stories, the through line here, is that some people, many people, are wound tight. And these folks don't know how tight they are wound. We used to call this "anger management issues," but today these issues are put under the rubric of emotional intelligence. I really don't think my father knew how hot he would get, or what triggered his rage, or whether it was justified. With all these stories, the anger feeds on itself. Control is not an option; you ride the anger wave until it subsides. Instead, we must know when the anger is coming (know your triggers) and be able to avoid it and control it.

Emotionally intelligent people are very in tune with their own emotions and how their own emotions affect others. Emotionally literate people can "read" the emotional state of those around them; they are in tune with their body language, tone, pitch of voice, eye contact, and emotional space. Emotional intelligence is an exploding "new front" in my work, and I am fascinated on where this side of my field will add value to corporate America.

Emotionally illiterate people are either not in touch with their own emotions, or the emotions of those they work with, or worse, don't care. Emotionally illiterate people lack the interpersonal self-awareness and don't understand why they have so many problems with relationships. Emotional Intelligence as an emerging field of study crossed my professional path when I read Daniel Goleman's "Emotional Intelligence, Why it can matter more than I.Q." Daniel Goleman is a journalist and I truly enjoyed his book and my field has embraced Emotional Intelligence for the value it brings to our organizational work.

I really like the most recent definition of Emotional Intelligence I could find and it comes from Athanasios S. Drigas and Chara Papoutsi in their article "A New Layered Model on Emotional Intelligence where they say "Emotional Intelligence is the ability to identify, understand, and use emotions positively to manage anxiety, communicate well, empathize, overcome issues, solve problems, and manage conflicts."[2]

In Goleman's book he talks about the Competencies of Being Emotionally Intelligent.[3]

1. **Emotional Self Control**—"rein in emotional impulse"
2. **Awareness of Others**—"to read another's innermost feelings"
3. **Managing Relationships**—"to handle relationships smoothly"

All the stories in this chapter and throughout this book show individuals who are not in tune with their own emotions. Their disrespectful, insulting comments, anger, or rage are also not in touch with how their comments and actions are affecting the people around them. Again, these individuals don't care or, even worse, are trying to elicit a response, a reaction of surprise, horror or—God help us—laughter. "Oh, I was just joking; don't get so worked up" when they are trying to provoke people in their circle of influence.

From the interviews I conducted for this book, I learned that toxic behaviors come from people with a lack of self-awareness. They have low to nonexistent emotional intelligence (emotionally illiterate); this coupled with the toxic person having power, being a senior person, or being a leader is a recipe for disaster. Because no one wants to tell the boss (or the family member) they are a jerk, people just look the other way, try to ignore said toxic conduct, and hope it goes away by itself or, worse, they just quit and who is left (in the organization)? The toxic person and their behaviors.

Journal: What are your triggers? What sets you off to where you just launch into a fit of anger?

CHAPTER 4.

THE CEO GRABBER—DRUNK WITH POWER

Almost everyone knows "The Grabber" in this client scenario. That person in power who makes the workplace their sexual playground. I was called in to coach a CEO "Grabber" by the vice president of human resources—who also happened to be related to the CEO. This is more common than you think with family-owned or closely held businesses.

Nobody wants to tell the person in power that they're toxic. People fear confrontation with their boss, and I understand that. So, many people hire a third party (like myself) to intervene. The problem is: hiring an outsider takes time and resources. I've seen these interventions take months or even years. During that time, people are suffering. Lots of hardworking people are chewed up and spit out.

You can do something now to get out in front of these issues. Yes, a third party may be required, but no matter what level you hold in the company, you can "skill up": learn how to be a part of the solution and not part of the problem (looking the other way and hoping these issues go away by themselves). You can learn skills, tools, and methods for addressing the toxicity and finding courage through knowledge. You can learn the same skills that us consultants possess.

THE GRABBER

The vice president of human resources had called me. "We have a very urgent matter; we need an Executive Coach specializing in Gender Equity and Harassment right away!"

"I'm your man. How can I help?"

The VP said, "Well, our CEO, his nickname is the Grabber. He hits on many of our younger female employees. He goes after anyone in a skirt." (It is rare to hear a woman say this, let alone a human resource executive.) "It is so bad that we actually have a slide in our new hire orientation warning employees: 'Don't be surprised if our CEO hits on you. He does not mean any harm. Just warning you!' Older men, you know?"

I was like, "Wait, what? It is in your New Hire Orientation Power Point slide deck? You actually warn your new hires before he harasses them?" This is what we call in our field "Having Prior Knowledge" and the risk for litigation, the amount of money in play, the numbers, the math, goes way up. I had not mentioned my rates yet to the client, and I quickly raised them in my mind before I shared them.

"The parties suing us got ahold of this slide deck."

"The parties suing you? How many?"

"At least nine. We are quite concerned this is going to turn out really bad for us. We want you to come in a coach our CEO one-on-one and then roll out harassment prevention training for the whole organization."

I asked the VP, "Gloves off or on?" She replied, "Bloody him. I want you to be the most direct, the most real, you can possibly be. He needs some really honest, tough love."

"On it. Anything else?"

"Yes, one more thing—I'm his wife."

"So let me get this straight. Your husband (and co-owner of the firm, they own it together) is harassing people all over the place, and no one is coming to you, the wife, VP of HR, to complain?"

"Correct."

A week later, I was pulling in and parking in front of the client's office building (they owned and occupied the whole building and employed several hundred people I'd been told).

As I am walking to the office through the parking lot, I see her, a '67 Corvette parked right in front with a name on a little sign in front of the car. Candy-apple red with a white top. Just gorgeous. With what looks like an inch of clear coat on the paint. Just shining in that sun. Just gorgeous. And whose name is on the sign? The CEO I am about to go coach one-on-one. I walk in and introduce myself.

"Oh, they're waiting for you. Let me show you to his office."

As I enter this big office, there he is behind a big desk and his wife is nearby, sitting at a conference table with the most serious look on her face, with a stare like lasers just burning a hole in her husband's face.

"Did you see it? My baby?" First thing out of his mouth.

"Excuse me? Oh, the '67 Corvette. Yes, I saw it, and it is not yours anymore."

"What?"

"You are being sued by a bunch of your employees for sexual harassment and possibly sexual discrimination, correct?"

"Well, yes."

"They have the New Hire Orientation Power Point Slide Deck where employees are warned that 'Our CEO, the Grabber' is coming for you!"

"Yes," he says with a smile and an odd giggle or whimper.

"Well, let me address your smile. This smug, almost cocky look you have on your face right now! Since you are a co-owner of this firm, the plaintiffs will pierce the corporate ownership veil of your firm, and they will go after your personal assets. They are going to gut you like a fish and go after all your assets. Let's see...nine plaintiffs, maybe more, will cost you millions! You have that much? Everything you have worked for—you just flushed it all down the toilet. That Vette out front, gone, will be sold at auction. You have a beach house? Boat maybe? All will be sold at auction at pennies on the dollar. All gone. You are an idiot!"

No one had ever spoken to him like this before. He was shocked.

He looked at his wife, who was looking at him with the same consistent stare, and he said to her, "I had no idea. I am so sorry, honey." No longer smiling, I might add. He wanted us to believe "he had no idea he was the source of all their toxic problems and issues" and not to mention it was going to cost their company a lot of money, money I don't think they had.

Needless to say, he took the rest of our coaching session very seriously, and his wife and VP of HR thanked me later. When the toxicity, the horrible behaviors, the CEO's conduct, is supported, is endorsed by the organization, look out. The penalty, the settlement money potential can be sky-high. The organization knew of his conduct and willingly let him run roughshod over all the employees.

Over and over again in the interviews people shared with me for this book, I heard "we know who these folks are and the higher they are up in the organization, the more likely we will ignore or look the other way." This is borderline negligence. They can't argue "we had no idea." In fact, some people, many people, including senior leaders, watched and said nothing.

This man was intoxicated by the power he held. He felt he could do anything he wanted. I felt like a million dollars walking out of that meeting. I was able to tell him what nobody else could (or would). I walked back to my car and knew I was doing right by all the people he had victimized. How many people would now be spared his sexist wrath? But I—and other coaches and trainers like me—can't be the only fighters in this battle. We need more agents of change, folks who step in, lean in, and don't suffer silently.

It is important to understand the concepts of power dynamics in the workplace. How people influence each other and the inherent structures in the workplace are very relevant here and throughout this book. The power between individuals and groups provides a context, a backdrop for this book. We are talking about more than authority or control; this backdrop includes the less clear concepts of dominance, privilege (not popular for many who have it), and how we communicate, our styles of communication.

There are, however, people in power who can change. I have met them, coached them, trained them. I watched the light bulb go off in this CEO's head while we had a heated conversation in his office. It took a very direct third party, a coach, a truth teller, to speak truth to power and get him to "see the light."

In the interviews I conducted for this book, so many of the interviewees told me no one inside the organization wanted to tell the CEO how they and specifically their actions were problematic, risky, and possibly illegal.

Journal: Have you ever worked in such a ridiculously horrible, toxic workplace? What did you do? Did you just leave, or did you stay and fight?

"BENIGN NEGLECT"

"Hey, I am told you are the top person to talk to about this." Just out of nowhere he calls me. We have never met or talked before, but I'm game; let's see where this conversation goes. He goes on to tell me he is the CEO of a 100-employee technology company.

"We are all White, and we serve a customer base that is 40 percent non-White. We are going through a hiring spurt, and we will be doubling in size this year." It is rare for a CEO to use these words, paint a picture in such direct racial terms. He seems sincere, genuine to me, over the telephone.

"Okay, I think I am following you here. I am listening."

"Well, you see, here is the problem. I know we are going to hire some non-White folk. I would like to hire people from the 40 percent of our customer base that I suspect we are underserving."

"Okay, all right, I follow you. Wow, you are really putting it out there in simple terms."

"On my executive team I have two very close buddies. They have been with me since I rose to the level of CEO. Now one of my buddies is a racist and the other is a sexist."

"Wait, how do you know?"

"They tell the most awful jokes and stories before, during, and after our executive team meetings. That is the first problem, but what is worse, as I reflect back over the years, I have never called them out. I typically smile, giggle, or even laugh at their ridiculous jokes and stories."

"The racist and sexist ones?"

"Yes. I am sorry to say. I would describe my posture here as benign neglect up until this point, this call to you today."

"Okay, so how can I help?" His brutal honesty is refreshing, quite frankly. He called me, a total stranger, to bare his soul, so to speak. I felt it was almost like a confession (I was raised a Catholic).

"I think, rather, I want to fire both of them today after this call and send a message that I, that this company, will no longer tolerate such racist and sexist comments, behaviors, stories, etc. I mean, we are going to hire people who will not find these comments amusing, respectful, or civil, let alone work-related."

"Do you think some of your employees are already upset about the racist and sexist comments and your lack of action to hold them accountable? I mean, you are the CEO; maybe they are afraid to come to you, to say anything."

"That has crossed my mind but regardless, I must act now, today. What do you think?"

"I recommend that first you apologize to all of your employees who have been present who have witnessed the sexist and racist comments and stories. Apologize for not being offended, for not thinking of their feelings, for not being sensitive, for really being so insensitive for far too long. Be vulnerable, be authentic, be genuine, and your employees will stand by you. Yes, fire your two colleagues, but I think you have to go further. We must create a new and better corporate culture and environment, one built on respect and dignity for all. A culture that values the diversity of all your employees and includes all, is inclusive of all. Your people will trust you more going forward, and we all work harder for someone we trust."

I ended by saying, "Happy to partner with you. I will take a bullet for you. Your brutal honesty is refreshing. It takes courage and self-reflection to call me, someone you don't know, and run this by me. I appreciate you, your call, and your time. Happy to help in any way I can."

Honesty, brutal honesty, is refreshing. Again, the power of being a third party, objective (I have no skin in his game), and being a good listener and sounding board can be clarifying for this CEO and so powerful and uplifting for me and almost transformational for us both; it's a win-win. This CEO was brutally honest with himself and with me, of course, and then genuinely wanted to know my opinion (from a stranger, I guess, who he thought was an expert on these matters).

You can be the person who turns on the light bulb sooner. The CEO in this instance was in denial for years. He had little to no self-awareness of the impact of his toxic colleagues—and no one said anything. Without intervention, this CEO would likely have continued to allow this toxic behavior to poison the culture of his organization.

In these stories, the CEOs were powerful and they were self-unaware, in denial (they knew how terrible they were), or just did not care because they were "drunk with power and felt they were above the rules and laws." Also, the power dynamics were in their favor: "I am the

CEO, I can do whatever I want." I think it is helpful here to provide some research-based context.

From a Harvard Business Review article entitled "What Self-Awareness Really Is (and How to Cultivate It)" by Tasha Eurich, I found this distinction Tasha makes very helpful. Tasha says, "Research suggests that when we see ourselves clearly, we are more confident and more creative. We make sounder decisions, build stronger relationships, and communicate more effectively. We're less likely to lie, cheat, and steal. We are better workers who get more promotions. And we're more-effective leaders with more-satisfied employees and more-profitable companies." She goes on to say, "For the last fifty years, researchers have used varying definitions of self-awareness. For example, some see it as the ability to monitor our inner world, whereas others label it as a temporary state of self-consciousness. Still others describe it as the difference between how we see ourselves and how others see us."[1] This last definition fits best for me; it rings clearest for me.

The gap between how I see myself and how others I interact with see me is spot-on. So often, I am brought into a situation and the gap is enormous and I am hired to close that gap. In my interviews, this was a theme: the narcissist CEO or senior executive who is this bull in a china shop with the lights off. As an executive coach, I would come along and turn the lights on.

The first step to deal with a toxic person in power is not to assess all the people involved but to make the toxic person understand themself first (take a hard look at yourself in the mirror).

Journal: This kind of honesty is rare. Have you ever seen it?

TOXICITY SELF-ASSESSMENT—ARE YOU BEING HONEST WITH YOURSELF?

What these stories show is narcissism at play. A new definition that fascinates me from the field committed to understanding narcissism, tells us that "People with narcissism "may be grandiose or self-loathing, extraverted or socially isolated, captains of industry or unable to maintain steady employment, model citizens or prone to antisocial activities," (from Scientific American).[2] What really hits me here is this research and all related focus on this 'lack of empathy for others' coupled with the power dynamics at play.

Power dynamics in a relationship can go one of three ways: demand/withdrawal (one party believes the other party does not understand or meet their interests, needs, or demands and they don't care), distancer/pursuer (one party is putting distance between to avoid closeness, understanding, and intimacy), and fear/shame (one party exhibits fear or insecurity and the other party blames themself and feels shame). Changing the power dynamic in your relationship requires a great deal of self-awareness, trust in those around you to give you the straight up feedback, vulnerability in owning your actions, and honest and respectful communication between all parties.

Ask yourself first, more importantly, regularly ask the people around you, people you work with and interact with every day, these questions about you. These can be challenging questions, the answers revealing. Compare what you think about yourself with what your colleagues and direct reports tell you. Is there a gap? If so, you must close that gap.

- Am I negative person? Ask around.
- Do I gossip about others not present? (gossip is rarely positive)
- Do I complain to others about things outside of my control?
- Do people come to me to gripe and share their negative perspectives and gossip about others?
- Am I attracted to more toxic, negative people?
- Do I allow my personal life to creep into the workplace and bring everyone else down?
- Do I derive joy from sharing my negative thoughts about others?
- Do I bring up stuff that happened in the past, unresolved issues, or issues not resolved to my liking years and years later?
- Do I contribute to a negative, hostile, hate-inspired culture and environment with my comments and actions and especially gossip?
- Do I really not care about the people I work with?

OR
- Am I an upbeat person, a positive person?
- Do I convey a positive self-image?
- Do I praise those around me?
- Do I always look for something positive to say to brighten up someone else's day?
- Do people come to me to ask for my counsel, advice on solving problems, or resolving conflict?
- Do I surround myself with positive people?
- Do I smile a lot?
- Am I attracted to positive, encouraging, supportive people?
- Do I call out negativity, toxicity, and hate?
- Do I care about the people I work with?

The first step in this journey to handling toxicity in a more effective and productive manner is to raise your self-awareness and then the next step is understanding how your actions affect others, the consequences, the impact of your actions on others.

"We are free to choose our actions...but we are not free to choose the consequences of these actions." —Stephen R. Covey.[3]

I am a behaviorist. I distill everything I do down to a set of behaviors, actions, and the consequences of those actions. This goes back to my days in college as a psychology and economics double major. We call it "Shaping Behavior."

Shaping behavior is about breaking down complex patterns of behavior into a specific, objective, measurable, and achievable set of specific behaviors. This is my approach or my methodology. In my executive coaching practice, I don't believe I change anyone. I create an environment where they choose to change themselves, one behavior at a time.

As you read my stories, go through them, and connect with them, you have to start asking yourself some questions. *Have I been in these situations? Do I resemble any of the parties in these stories?* The "Prefers and the Nevers" is my approach, my method for distilling toxic people and their behaviors down to the simplest, most rudimentary set of behaviors.

THE PREFERS AND THE NEVERS

One very simple and powerful approach or technique is to distill all behaviors down to a set of behaviors (at home or in the workplace) <u>you want to see every day,</u>

your **PREFERS**, and the behaviors you don't want to see, ever, your **NEVERS**. At home, you could have a family meeting. Any group from your job to your family to a bible study: what are the behaviors that contribute to positive interaction in our group and camaraderie, and what behaviors discourage us from coming and participating (today it might be political polarization). You can point out that we are not singling out any person but rather separating individuals from their conduct, their comments and behaviors, and focusing on said behaviors (and the consequences of those behaviors per se).

You can meet with your colleagues at work and say, "Look there are behaviors (I see, I experience, that I am subject to) that create and support a very positive, welcoming, healthy, productive work environment. Then there are behaviors that suck the oxygen out of the room, kill morale, and are toxic, and I never ever want to see or experience them again."

Grab an easel with paper and draw a T-chart. On the left, label for the NEVERS, the behaviors that we never want to see again. On the right, label for the PREFERS, the behaviors we all prefer to see. Hopefully, those individuals who see comments and behaviors that they resemble will take notice, right? "Hey, they are talking about me" without actually embarrassing them. This can be reactive or proactive: you see a pattern of escalating behaviors and you react to stop them with this methodology. But this method is also proactive because it might prevent behaviors you don't want to wait and see happen in your workplace in the future.

Here is a list to help you get started and to generate ideas.

NEVERS

"Not my job" (before you have even asked them anything specific)

"Above my pay grade"

"Outside my swim lane"

Love to say "Look what the cat dragged in?"

Gossip about others not present (manipulative)

Have meetings before and after your meetings to undermine your meetings

Undermining colleagues, backstabbing

Convey you really don't care about others

Meet with parents separately and play them against each other; I also call this "shopping for the right answer"

You are seen as notoriously problematic, full of drama, prickly at best, toxic when in your full glory

Have real problems with people who are different, behavior that is sexist, racist, homophobic, intolerant of other religions, for example

Being disrespectful, condescending to any or all

PREFERS

"How can I help?"

"How are you doing?"

"You okay? You good?"

"Can I lend a hand?"

Encouraging, supportive, positive behaviors

Only talking about people present

Embracing change positively

Convey you care, your reputation is you are a positive, go-to person

Meet with parents together to present a problem, root cause, and solutions

Welcoming, inclusive of everyone: a stranger is just someone they have not met

You are a good listener, people gravitate toward you for positive counsel, advice

Being respectful to each other, honoring the dignity of all

As long as you stay focused on sets of behaviors (no names), this can be a very powerful technique. Take the T-chart you created and post it somewhere public, in the break room, for example, and people can add to it (leave a marker). This becomes an organic, living document where we hold each other accountable to a set of behaviors.

Now if your organization, your employer, has a set of core values or guiding principles, you can note the relevant core values/principles that we are living and honoring, or that we are dishonoring and not living. This really anchors the behaviors and helps you all create the right working environment and a healthy culture.

I have found in my personal life too many people behave in a toxic way and play dumb. Nobody says anything to them, allowing them to become a worse and worse version of themselves. So many choose to be conflict avoiders and unintentionally "feed the monster" because the toxic person and their behaviors are tacitly supported by our lack of action. *No one is saying anything, so they must be okay with my actions.*

Also, I have observed too many people don't get involved; they stay on the sidelines. In school, if you are not being bullied, if you are not the object or target of the bully, you don't get involved. *Better this person than me.* Bullies thrive in this environment.

Interviewing people for this book from many sectors told me that we often know who the toxic people and what their actions are, but we are not skilled to acknowledge and address the toxicity. Some call it a lack of courage, some call it indifference; it is both and more. If you don't have the skills to engage the toxicity, then you don't believe in yourself, and this contributes to the lack of courage so many describe. The interviews also pointed out too many people on the sidelines; no one wants to get involved, so the conflict, the toxicity, lives on.

The old adage comes racing back into my mind: "See something, say something." But so many people, most people, are conflict avoiders and look the other way; they leave the room, pretend like nothing happened, and hope "these issues just go away by themselves."

This is even more true at home. When I am working with a client and they say, "We are like a family here," I shudder at the thought. Many, if not most, families can be terribly dysfunctional, and the toxicity at home sometimes rivals the toxicity at the work. I want this book to help you not only at work but also at home, so we continue to look at issues at home in the next chapter.

CHAPTER 5.

HOME FRONT HAS BECOME MORE TOXIC

Civility is gone. Current events, violence, crime, guns, the volatile political environment, in an election year no less, what news media reports has made being a toxic person and your toxic behaviors almost normal, almost hip. Like being a jerk is okay, cool, so many wear it on their sleeve like a badge of honor. Some forces within the media will have you believe you are a "snowflake" if you show any sensitivity or understanding for people in difficult situations. Throw in COVID, and we are off to the toxic races.

This book is about not allowing the toxicity at home or work (or church) to become "the new normal." For some, unfortunately, toxicity at home dwarfs toxicity at work. We must go back to civility, decency, respect, dignity for all in all aspects of our life. I remember when family time—Thanksgiving, Christmas—was revered, respected, protected time. Now, all I hear are people "dreading the holidays."

DREADING THE HOLIDAYS

One the most toxic moments I have ever experienced was a particularly memorable Christmas party at our house. Snow was falling on a crisp but not frigid night (perfect for sledding). The whole family was invited. All three of the siblings, my folks, and all of our kids were present. As usual, I had a warm fire burning in the fireplace. I chop my own wood, no gas fireplaces at our house. Kids were getting ready to go out and sled. Such a cozy, loving, holiday vibe was present, uplifting, almost spiritual. Like something out of a Hallmark movie. It was going to be a perfect night (I thought and whispered to Kelly).

Then it all came to a screeching halt when my mom and dad walked up to Kelly and me. We were in the den in front of the fire talking about the joyous spirit of the night. My mom leaned in (my father right there in tow, next to her) and asked Kelly, "Mauricio can do so much better than you. When are you leaving him?"

Her words hit me like a ton of bricks. I did not take it well. I raised my voice so all in the room could hear me and no one could be in denial, no one could pretend they did not hear what my mom said. Repeat what you hear; sometimes people don't know they are thinking out loud.

"Oh, I did *not* just hear you say that."

Yes, use volume, raise your voice to shame if you have to (not the first time this has happened) and don't let anyone play the denial game.

"Unbelievable! You just asked Kelly, in front of me, *my son can do so much better than you, when are you leaving him? Unbelievable! Really?*"

I looked at Kelly. "So sorry you just heard that."

I had sent ahead the Christmas family party email with ground rules, norms, and code of conduct: be positive, be respectful tonight, no drama at my party or don't come.

Also, I have to note, by this point in our marriage, we had three small kids (hoping they were not present watching this toxic drama unfolding in front of everyone).

I heard more than one anonymous "Mama!"

I guided my mom with my hand on the small of her back and said, "Let's go." I looked at my dad and said, "Papa, and you, you just stand there and watch Mama just torch the place. Let's go." We were headed to the front door. Kelly was already at the front door holding it open.

"Nice to see you Mr. and Mrs. Velásquez. Merry Christmas, happy holidays!"

I escorted my mom and dad down my long driveway. It was cold out (snow was on the ground and falling), but I did not feel the cold. I was feeling a mix of emotions, anger but also sadness. We had been down this road many times. I would warn my mother, and she would say and do things regardless of my advice.

My mom was so surprised. "What is happening here? What did I say? Why are you so upset?"

"Are you kidding me? Mama, actions have consequences, and you just said one of the most hateful, disgusting, anti-family comments that I could not even imagine would come out of your mouth."

"Oh Mauricio, stop being so dramatic, so sensitive," she said. "I was just kidding; I did not mean it."

I was so ready to lose it, but I kept my composure. I looked at Mom in disbelief and bewilderment. I was trying to stay in control, to not lose my temper, but I was really boiling over inside with frustrated rage.

I said to her, "You know, you raised me with the phrase 'if you have nothing positive to say, don't say it.' What has happened to you?"

Mama retorted, "Oh, don't bring that up. This is what happens when I have a son who is a diversity trainer."

"Wait, what? Are you trying to blame me here? Mama, your words hurt me, hurt Kelly. And in front of the whole family, no less. And how about the kids? Hearing Abuela (grandma) saying this to their mother? You are putting me in a horrible situation. You are asking me to choose between you and Kelly. I choose Kelly! I would like to sleep in my bed tonight. If I don't kick you out right now, there will be consequences for me." My mom still looked confused.

I sighed. "Do you know what Maya asked me tonight? 'Why does Abuela not like Mom?'" Maya was very young, single digits at the time.

That seemed to finally get through to her. My mom exclaimed, "What?"

"Mama, I love you very much. I am your firstborn. I tend to be the truth teller in our family. You are not fooling anyone; you are not subtle. You have to stop making faces and rolling your eyes when Kelly talks. You have to stop leaving the room when Kelly enters the room. You are in her house, she is cooking you and all of us a gourmet meal, reflecting hours of work and preparation. I tell you all of this because I love you; I could just kick you out and you would have no idea what is happening. I could have kicked you out and slammed the front door, but I wanted to explain to you that you have done. I wanted you to understand."

Mama was still muttering, "I can't believe this is such a big deal." My father was just standing there grabbing my mom and telling her, "We have to go."

At this point I was so frustrated with my parents, and I didn't think my mom was getting it. And I didn't want to relive this horror show, so I went all in. I mean, I have to walk back into my house and face Kelly and the kids. *We are going to DEFCON 1*, I say to myself. At this point, I put it all out there on the table.

"Okay, Mama, this friction, this drama, this is not the first time we have been here but it will be the last time." *For a while,* I think. Mama and Papa look at me intently.

"I am banning both of you from my house, from any visits for six months. I will change the locks, change my mobile number if I have to, but you are *not welcome here* for at least six months. Now leave, please!" I turned and walked away.

Can I tell you, the next six months were some of the most glorious months of my life. My blood pressure went down, the sun was brighter, the food tasted better, our marriage flourished.

My mom would text or try to call (I would not take her calls), and it was always something to the effect of not seeing and missing the grandchildren. And, of course, my mom would involve my brother and sister. At first, I conveyed it through them but eventually (months later) I told her directly.

"You want to see my kids, you must first apologize to Kelly, their mother, personally, and to the whole family on a big group call. When you disrespect my wife in front of the whole family, I feel it is a personal affront, a personal attack on me. I would prefer you apologize to Kelly in front of the whole family."

That never happened. I might add that I almost extended the ban to a year. However, my mom did stop being so blatantly toxic from that day forward. I would also add that I think Kelly truly appreciated me honoring her, supporting her, defending her so to speak. This story of all of them is my flashpoint, my tipping point from inaction to action with full, long-term consequences. My marriage was clearly suffering when my mom would come over and make these little comments. I described it as "throwing grenades into my home."

Participants in my workshops have often commented, "You had guts to stand up to your mom. That must have taken some courage."

Guts? I had to choose, right? I was more interested in honoring and supporting Kelly. I guess if I watched and did nothing (like most people in dysfunctional families) I might fear Kelly saying, "Why did you not stand up for me?" But it was so clear to me I had to act, I had to say and do something immediately: my kids, my whole family was watching (including the other spouses in our family).

It was like the floor opened when my parents were disrespectful (toxic) and they were sucked out of the house to never be seen again that night.

I was actually quite surprised at myself: I moved quickly, no pause, to remove my parents from my house. I love them, but I can also call out their behaviors and show them that their behaviors have consequences. Love the person, dislike the behavior.

In my interviews and, quite frankly, in my workshops (over nearly thirty years now) many people have told me: "I don't have your courage or your skills." I more often get, "What typically happens in my house is catastrophe unfolds, everybody watches, says nothing, then we move on, ignoring any consequences." And yes, people will talk about these incidences for years to come afterward.

Most families have very long memories and long-term damaged feelings.

Update: Kelly invited Mama over for Thanksgiving recently (my father has passed away) and Mama was very respectful, very positive, very measured. Of course, I watched over the whole week like a lifeguard up on a stand with a whistle, making sure it went smoothly. We had a good time. The whole Thanksgiving week was quite enjoyable. It can happen; civility and decency are so much richer, healthier emotions than bitterness and anger.

Journal: This is one of the most popular stories I recite in my workshops that resonates with participants. "Happened to me or I have been there" are the most common comments. Have you been here before?

DON'T EVEN GET ME STARTED ON POLITICS

Politics are not discussed at family gatherings at my home. I send out an email ahead of any major family event, typically "Rules of Engagement" which contains what food to bring or not bring, the menu, etc. What are off-limits: politics, COVID (yes, we had disagreements about the vaccine), and religion, too. Hey, you are spiritual, religious, have faith, that's okay by me, but to impose it on others, to judge others, "you are going to hell and all that"? Ah, no. Of course, some family members want to discuss politics with that same religious zeal. Ah, no, not in my house.

Some families just need a little structure; define the consequences right up front and there is no mystery when someone "goes off the respectful yellow brick road" and they are escorted out of my house.

In my interviews and in my workshops, I hear that this just does not happen: pointing out to family members that their actions have consequences and then enforcing those consequences is very rare. Most families just grin and bear it and talk about for years to come.

BIBLE STUDY OR HATE GROUP?

I truly enjoy being active in my church. At one time I was asked to be a lay leader in my church, and this gave me some insight into church affairs. Actually, you are only supposed to be a lay leader for four years, and I was asked or rather given an extension to serve eight years. I really enjoyed that experience. Between monthly lay leader meetings and weekly bible study, it was challenging to meet all of those commitments because I traveled a lot, but I tried to make it work.

It was a workout, a real challenge to go every week to get to this bible study, but I was committed. Traffic is always tricky to navigate, and I cannot stand just sitting there in traffic. On this particular evening, I was actually early, which is very rare for me. As I sat down (with an attentive smile), I just started listening to what my colleagues were saying and talking about: news of the day, current events. To my surprise, it was ugly. They were bashing Democrats and Catholics and well, I could not just sit there, I had to say something. They just kept going and going and feeding off each other (toxicity run rampant).

So, I said when there was a break, a pause in the ranting and raving, "Wow, I did not know this was a hate group. I mean, I resemble your remarks, this is very troubling to me." I stood up and walked out. As I headed home, I called our pastor and I told him, "You know it takes a great deal of effort and time on my part to go to this bible study group, and what did I find tonight? I was surrounded by toxicity, negativity, horrible labeling and stereotyping."

In the next Sunday service, our pastor, our reverend, called out my bible study brothers and sisters anonymously by focusing just on their toxic behaviors and actions. I will never forget our reverend had an interesting opening to this conversation:

"You know what it means to be Christian. It means to be Christlike. The old adage of what would Jesus do (WWJD)."

He had the whole congregation's attention immediately.

Our reverend gave this example. "We need to pray for 'Mauricio and Kelly' is very Christian. What happened? Tell us more. Not so Christian." He went on to talk about gossip, hearsay, backstabbing, labeling, racism, sexism, ethnocentrism, stereotyping groups you don't like "as not Christian at all."

I could feel my bible study brothers and sisters looking at me with lasers for eyes, and I looked right back at them (why should I be afraid or embarrassed?). *He is talking about you; you should be ashamed of yourselves!* Shame can be a very powerful dynamic, especially in church.

Needless to say, I never went back to that bible study group. I will share that a few of the members did come up to me later and apologize. It takes a very big person to be called out, own it, and apologize after the fact. The toxic behaviors must be called out and confronted. Maybe even especially at church. Too many of us sit and watch and say nothing and the conflict avoidance is interpreted as tacit support. We must all go from bystander to upstander in all facets of our lives. Especially if your children are present and watching you! Lead by example.

I learned that even in the most "holy of places" there can be disrespect and toxicity and that we must not watch idly by. We cannot freeze and smile to go along: we must call it out. I also don't think it is Christian or Christlike to hate so much and to spread hate through rumor in, say, a bible study group.

I have no doubt that rudeness, disrespect, incivility, and toxicity are all way up in our society. This is exactly why I wrote this book. So many watch, stand by, and say nothing. I think social media and traditional media home in on these stories. You hear about the horrible things being said and done, but where is the outrage? Where is the response?

A great article caught my eye. Entitled "It's Not News That Incivility Is on the Rise, but What Do We Do about It?" really positions this topic quite nicely. Author Julie Asher starts by quoting a recent *New York Times* headline, "Rudeness is on the rise. You got a problem with that?" Asher highlights a recent LinkedIn article, "How rude behavior is becoming the new normal in America." Yet another headline from *Fortune* espouses: "It's not just you, people really are being more rude lately." Add "that the majority of Americans polled on the topic say, that the 'tone and civility of US political debate' has been worsening for some time," we are all seeing emerging decay of civility in our society, and it is why I wrote this book.[1]

We know what the toxic behaviors and actions are, they make the news, but there is no mention of what people are doing to stop it from becoming the new normal. We need to skill people up, empower as many people as we can to fight back, to push back against the lack of civility, the disrespect, the hatred, the toxicity.

Journal: I know this might be controversial, but I will not shy away from toxic behaviors in all aspects of our lives. Have you seen toxicity at church?

STOP-START

This is one of the most powerful techniques I have ever come across in my career, and I use this technique every day. I will keep saying this throughout the book, with this and other techniques: you must separate the person from their behavior and focus your efforts on their toxic behaviors, their actions, their toxicity, and the consequences, the impact of these actions on people present and of course on the organization or the family as a whole.

The only way to become effective at using this technique is to use it, practice it, and apply it every day in all aspects of your life because it is a relevant, pertinent, highly applicable technique. This technique comes from marriage counseling that addresses spousal abuse. Many years ago, I volunteered in a women's shelter for victims of intimate partner violence in Louisa County, Virginia. This experience had a profound effect on me, my role, and my expectations of my role as a consultant, trainer, coach, husband and father, and of course the writing of this book. This is like a script; always follow the script.

This technique works if you use it, practice it—in essence, master it. It has two benefits: First, when you speak your mind intrinsically, you feel better when the words come out of your mouth. The second benefit is that it is also powerful when the "words land on the other person" and they hear it and adjust their behaviors accordingly.

Start with a Positive

Please stop _____
(describe negative/unproductive behavior)

Start _____
(describe new, more appropriate/positive behavior)

Continue _____
(describe ongoing positive behavior)

End with a Positive

First, you start with a positive (+)

Please **STOP** _____ (describe negative, hateful, toxic behavior)

Please **START** _____ (describe alternate more positive behavior, better, more productive, more respectful)

CONTINUE _____ (describe a previous positive behavior you have seen)

End with a positive (+)

It is called a "feedback sandwich" because you always start and end with a positive: that makes it easier to use, to be understood, and "easier to consume or digest the feedback."

Here are some starters that are positive.

STARTERS AT WORK
"You are one of our top performers."
"You are a valuable member of our team."

"People look up to you!"
"People respect you!"
"You are a highly influential person on our team/in our department."
"I respect you, I value you."

STARTERS AT HOME
"You know I love you very much."
"You are family; we are in this together for life."

NEUTRAL STARTERS (Work/Home) Here are more neutral starters but they also work.
"You and I go way back."
"We have worked side by side for many years."
"I know we can do better; our relationship can be on more solid footing."
"We are family, our children look up to us; we can help each other, learn from each other."

I felt the best approach here was just to give you a bunch of powerful examples and then you can "utilize the technique to fit your toxic situation." I give you examples for at work, at home, at school, etc.

AT WORK/HOME
Start with a POSITIVE
"People listen to you and come to you. You are influential on our team or in this department." (Positive, fact)
    OR
"We have known each other a long time." (Neutral, fact, implies we have a decent relationship.)
1. Please **STOP** *being negative all the time.*

2. Please **STOP** *gossiping about other people* (negativity implied), especially when they are not present (wondering what this person says about me).
3. Please **STOP** *fighting change, challenging new policies and procedures.*
4. Please **STOP** *trying to preserve the status quo.*
5. Please **STOP** *being problem-oriented, always focusing on the problem.*
6. Please **STOP** *dragging down the whole team with your focus on problems.*

1. Please **START** *being more positive, more constructive.*
2. Please **START** *talking only about people who are present; please be positive.*
3. Please **START** *embracing change, understanding why change is imperative.*
4. Please **START** *focusing on how we can change, what we can change, what we must change.*
5. Please **START** *focusing on a future state, an ideal state that is better, more effective, more positive, more respectful.*
6. Please **START** *being solutions-oriented, focusing on root cause(s) and solutions.*

1–6 **CONTINUE** *to give this organization 110 percent.*

1–6 **CONTINUE** *to be fully committed to this organization.*

1–6 **CONTINUE** *to work so very hard.*

1, 2, 4 **CONTINUE** *to be so committed to this family, our family, our church, our school.*

End with a POSITIVE
"You are a valued member of our team."
"You are a role model, and I want you to model the best behavior."
"This whole family looks up to you."

Now for some situations that you have might have experienced.

<u>Uber Driver</u>
I am a big fan of Uber and how much value Uber has added to my life. (+)
Please *stop* just sitting there and expecting a nice tip.
Please *start* helping me with my luggage; it is heavy, and helping will earn the tip you want.
Continue to listen to your customers.
Only telling you this because I know you want five stars. (+)

<u>Angry Server</u>
I love your food and the ambiance is great here. We come here all the time. (+)
(I was a server for many years.)
Please *stop* telling us you will be right back and then we don't see you for nearly one hour.
Please *start* telling us, giving us a reasonable expectation like "I will be back in five or ten minutes" and actually come back.
Continue to try your best; I see you hustling.
I get you are slammed, just be honest, tell the customer you are slammed. (+)

Office Gossip

You have worked here a long time, and you have much to teach me and others. (+)

Please *stop* gossiping all the time about new hires, who you think is sleeping with whom, etc.

Please *start* focusing more on your work, our work together, and what we have to accomplish.

Continue to work hard, teach and mentor others.

I tell you this because I think you can have a greater, more positive impact, on so many more people. (+)

Parenting 101

You are a good, hard-working student. (+)

Please *stop* telling me you are going to fail this class when you're in the first week of school.

Please *start* telling me how you will prepare, for example, find tutor, form study group.

Continue to work hard at school and bring a positive attitude to this class.

I know you can face this challenge and overcome it. (+)

Church Gossip

You know so many people in our congregation. (Neutral to +)

Please *stop* gossiping about our parishioners, especially with such personal matters.

Please *start* being more positive about our parishioners, only sharing, talking of the good, the uplifting news.

Continue to give this church your full commitment.

I want you to be known for helping others, not pulling them down or holding them back. (+)

Sexual Inappropriateness at Work

Look, you have worked here a long time, people respect you. (+)

Please *stop* commenting on how attractive you find the new hires.

Please *stop* commenting on what parts of their anatomy you like or don't like.

Please *start* focusing more on your work, your performance, your deadlines.

Continue to mentor others on how to do things correctly and professionally.

I tell you because I want you to continue to be successful here. (+)

Trying to Distract

I value your contributions to this company. (+)

Please *stop* talking about others and their work and contributions in a negative manner.

Please *start* talking about you, your work, your performance, your contributions.

Continue to give our organization your best effort.

I am only telling you this because I know you are capable enough to go to an even higher level of performance. (+)

Journal: Stop-Start is a very direct technique and can be used in all aspects of your life, in all toxic interactions. Try to draft or script your next interaction with a toxic person and their behaviors.

So many interviews I conducted for this book mentioned their supervisors and managers needed training, skills in how to address and how to engage toxic people and their behaviors. How to have difficult conversations is often about giving feedback to a toxic person. This chapter is where we really start to see, where I start to provide, very specific and concrete tips, tools, and techniques. A script so to speak for interpersonal communication, but also for written communication, in a note or email.

In my research for this book, I was intrigued by Christine Porath, associate professor at Georgetown University's McDonough School of Business (she has studied workplace incivility for the last twenty years), and I could not agree more with her comments.

Paraphrasing Christine Porath she writes: Incivility is like a virus you can catch anywhere—online, at work, in families, in our communities. We can see that people pass it on to others even when they're not aware of it and may not mean to demean others. It can be spread simply by someone 'who is on edge and just took in a lot of negativity and turns around and shouts at someone else.' This kind of disrespect, rudeness spreads. This is why our small actions matter so much.[2] She is spot on.

Over the course of my nearly thirty years of conducting workshops, doing workplace investigations, and the interviews for this book, I've learned that people are not skilled, not equipped, have no idea how to deal with difficult behaviors, toxic behaviors, toxic people. They often freeze like a deer in headlights. This Stop-Start Continue Technique is a life changer and can really make a difference if you use it. This technique is not a secret; some people are aware of it (social workers are taught this in their program), but too many don't use it, don't try it, or don't practice this technique, hence they never master the technique and maximize its effect on themselves or others.

This technique is applicable any time, all the time, anywhere, any place, as long as you have a set of visible, objective, measurable behaviors to work with, to utilize, to plug into this technique. There is so much toxicity out there and so many people being victimized and silently suffering. What if you could say something, do something that does not make the person you are speaking to, coaching really, defensive but rather help them understand how their actions, especially toxic actions, are affecting you?

Kelly and I were walking in a mall, and we came across an ugly sight. A man, possibly the father of this child, was hitting his daughter with his open hand in front of everybody. Most people watched in horror, but I had to say something; I could not just walk away and ignore what I'd just witnessed.

"Excuse me! You appear to be this person's guardian or parent. Yikes, ouch, you just hit your daughter here in public in front of all of us. Please stop hurting her, especially in public. Please start thinking about how embarrassing it is for the both of you, but especially the person you are hurting. Continue to care for this person, for their welfare. I know you are going to say 'this is none of your business' but you did this in public in front of many witnesses and that camera over there that has also recorded this incident. Please take care of each other."

I hope this chapter captured your attention on the "home front." Now let's look at some more workplace stories. Given current events and the political landscape being so tense and nasty, these toxic issues and related conversations will keep us on our toes.

CHAPTER 6.

WORKPLACE RIDDLED WITH TOXICITY

Warning—Racist Language in this chapter.

WORKPLACE TOXICITY CAN MAKE THE HOME TOXICITY LOOK LIKE A WALK IN THE PARK

"Being thrown under the bus" is one of the most common phrases I hear in my workshops. It's often about someone being disrespected but, more painfully, in front of other people, your colleagues, your peers. It is at that moment we are put to the test: am I going to just grin and bear it or say something? The following story is one of the most popular stories I use in my workshops; it has resonated, connected with so many people. Participants in my workshop just nod in approval or agreement.

THIS IS A NEED-TO-KNOW MEETING AND YOU DON'T NEED TO KNOW

In my first job after earning my master's in business administration from George Washington University, I worked hard to make a difference every day. I received what looked like an urgent email for a staff meeting hastily scheduled for later that day. I was the newest member of the human resource (HR) team, and I was still learning my way. The meeting had not started yet, but everyone was there.

My boss, the head of HR, Sara, looked up at me as I tried to take a seat. "What are you doing here?" she asked.

"Well," I answered, "I got your email."

"This is a need-to-know meeting, and you don't need to know." She dismissed me with the waving of her hand like I was a bothersome fly. As she looked back down at her document she added, "Bye."

I will never ever forget that moment. As I walked out, not one person could look me in the eye. Sara was famous for throwing anyone under the bus who called her out. We all feared her retaliatory fury. No one would come to my aid, not even make a face or say anything, let alone call her out. The embarrassing tension just dominated the moment.

I walked back to my cubicle furious, embarrassed, really tired, and just exhausted of her toxic antics. I had not been there a year yet, and I just could not take it anymore. I had my résumé ready, and I sat down at my cubicle and hit Send.

"Get in here," said Sara with a perturbed tone a few weeks later. My cubicle was next to hers. It was my last day, and Sara waited till the end of my last day to call me into her office. "I can't believe you're leaving me!" Mind you, everyone on the human resources team could hear or listen in on conversations when people raised their voice. Sara liked to her raise voice, often, and I obliged by raising my voice so all could hear.

"Sara," I said, "I asked around and I am the eighth person in this job in eleven years. Guess what we all have in common?" I raised my voice for sure, but I stayed steady, collected.

Sara said, "What?"

"You! Here is my exit interview: you suck, you are a terrible boss, a bully. Your actions, the way you treat any and all of us, is borderline abuse."

What did I have to lose? On my last day at the final hour (and I knew Sara would not give me a recommendation) I let her have it. It felt so good. I could see Sara's face getting flush. She was starting to crinkle her forehead, the telltale sign she was about to get enraged, about to blow like a volcano.

"I am so angry at you right now I could punch you!"

I am certain everyone was listening.

"Hit me as hard you can on my face, leave a mark, and I will call the police and get you on assault. You are a total nightmare to work for!" I walked out, head high, and never looked back. Sara did me a favor in a way: that was my last human resources job (internal) and that moment of toxicity put me on a path to start my own firm.

I could not think of working for another bad boss ever again. Speaking my piece and telling truth to power had never felt so good, so right, so spot-on. I will never forget that experience. Who knew back then it would be part of my book many years later? If you can't tell, this is almost like therapy for me.

I learned that I would not allow anyone to treat me this way. I would not stand for it and what others might tolerate or accept; I was just not going to have it. I guess my threshold for being bullied is low. Interviews I conducted for this book revealed that way too many managers and leaders look the other way, turn the other check, and that "power corrupts and absolute power corrupts absolutely." You can find the interview questions and answers summarized into themes at the back of the book.

By the way, this nightmare boss was let go six months later, and I threw a party and reached out to all of the alumni, people who had held my job before me. What a great time. We celebrated that justice had finally come to our former boss.

Now for a memorable investigation and coaching engagement. You are not going to believe this one.

THEY HIRED *YOU* TO COACH *ME*?

My client called me and asked me to conduct an investigation of the foreman of an asphalt plant and to follow it up with individual coaching for the foreman, the target or object of the investigation. Work at the plant is hot and dirty and can be very dangerous. The bulk of the workforce are Latino, and I speak Spanish. I checked in with all the employees, one-on-one, and tried to make it seem informal and relaxed. Sure enough, all the employees tell me the foreman does not address any of them by their names. Their names are on their uniform, by the way. I am told he is horrible, a bully, barks out orders, is very difficult, very hostile, and a racist. Some of the worst kind of toxic behaviors.

More than one interviewee tells me, "He is lucky we have not knifed him." The most common response to my inquiries includes: "He calls us 'Beaners' or 'Fxxxing Beaners' or 'Motherfxxxing Beaners.'" Beaner is an offensive term for someone of Mexican descent. I report to the client immediately that we have a potential situation for violence. I ask to meet with the foreman as soon as possible. The client makes him come to my office for the coaching session.

The first thing he said to me upon settling into my office was, "They hired *you* to coach *me*? A Beaner?"

Looking directly into his eyes, I smiled and said, "Oh, this is going to be easy. You just said that out loud, to me, the investigator, your coach? You just confirmed and corroborated my findings."

His smile grew. Oh, I wanted to remove that grin from his face so bad.

"Well, yeah," he answered. "I am who I am." I went on to ask him why he thought we were meeting, why his employer had hired me in the first place. "Look man, I am an old dog, and you can't teach an old dog new tricks." He admitted being a racist, his comments were racist, and that "management is okay with it. I mean, I get the job done."

"If they hired me, they are not okay with your racist comments. We will get you a kennel somewhere else." Old dog my ass. He was defiant, not apologetic, and it was clear he was not going to change. Rarely do I know someone's intentions. His intentions were clear: here was a toxic person who was not going to change. Almost like he wore his racism on his sleeve like a badge of honor. Like the workers deserved to be treated this way. Actions have consequences, I told him. He was putting his employer at risk of lawsuits and litigation.

In one ear, out the other. He did not seem to care. Now, as I dug deeper into the toxic issues at this plant, I learned that his boss, the plant manager, was also toxic and might have taught him everything he knew. His boss had mentored him, groomed him, modeled the inappropriate behavior, and given this person a safe place to be horrible to all. Possibly even protected him, advocated for him. Next to or behind most toxic people are their enablers, colluders, even mentors who taught them most of what they know.

My recommendation: terminate the foreman. He will continue to create a racially hostile workplace, and I fear an escalation to violence. He was abruptly fired, and I moved on to his boss. I met with the plant manager, and he definitely seemed perturbed that he had to meet with me. He did not know that his protégé was going to lose his job, but I went for the jugular with this guy. I cut to the point immediately. He was trying to justify his very toxic management and leadership style.

"So tell me about your son," I asked. "I understand he is autistic."

"How do you know that about my son?" he asked, shocked.

"Not important. Tell me, how do you feel when your son is bullied in school? The same behaviors that you exhibit with your employees." My wife is a speech pathologist and her clients include children on the autism spectrum.

"Wait, what?"

"I bet you can't stand it. I mean, you're probably furious when your son is treated horribly at school, bullied, talked down to, physically intimidated, all of that. Yet, here you are, treating your employees nearly the same way. Your behaviors are adolescent at best, racist and violence threatening at worst. Maybe you are projecting this anger on your employees; it really doesn't matter. I'm not here to diagnose you—I'm here to make sure you stop! How do you reconcile these two similar situations?"

He covered his face with his hands, lowered his head, and started crying uncontrollably. I just watched him quietly. That was my last conversation with him. I am told he changed his behaviors dramatically after our coaching session, and I know hearing that his "mini me" was let go drove home my points and ensured some level of behavior change. Nothing like seeing someone you manage get fired and understand it could happen to you next.

Now wait. This story is not over.

About three months later, I heard from the fired foreman. He called me out of the blue. "Mauricio, you have to help me. You know they fired me, right?"

"Yes," I replied, "I know something about that, and this *Beaner* has no interest in helping you!"

"Don't bring that up. Look, I need your help!" His voice was trembling. "They took my Harley, my boat, I can't make my mortgage payment. My wife has left me. I've been working at the plant since high school. I was making real good money, six figures. Well, when I got fired. I went to work for another place, and they started me near entry level. I mean, I am making like $25k. I can't make ends meet."

"So?" I asked.

"So, can you call back my last job and have them take me back?"

I said, "Oh no! I will not put my reputation on the line for you. You made your bed, now you have to sleep in it. Actions have consequences, and you did not feel or believe that this employer cared. Well, they care about their employees. Best of luck to you!" And I hung up.

Some people just don't get it. They don't get it mentally; it does not make sense to them that they have to change. They don't get it emotionally, in the heart; why do I have to change, to be more respectful, decent? Well, eventually the light bulb goes off: people get it when it hits them in the wallet. You know what they say: "money talks and bullshit walks."

In this situation, I felt empowered (by the client) to just be blunt with him. It felt good, almost righteous. I mean, come on, he is calling me a *Beaner* but months later wants me to help him? Ouch, I guess he was desperate, his world was crumbling all around him. Now I know somebody will say have a heart, can you forgive him?

I am a Christian and we talk about forgiveness, one of our main tenets. Is it my place to forgive him? Does he have remorse, or has he even forgiven himself? No. I think he is just driven by the almighty dollar, and he can't make ends meet. I felt bad for him, but did I forgive him? I don't think it is my place or that it even matters if I forgive him. To this day, I think about him: did he change? Did his heart change? I fear not.

Journal: Do you know somebody who did not "get it" until they lost their job? Then found it difficult to find a similar well-paying job?

THE I-MESSAGE

Giving feedback and responding (not reacting) to toxic behaviors and conduct is what this book is all about. Equipping you, skilling you up, so to speak. None of these techniques are taught in high school or college or graduate school in most areas of discipline. Attorneys know how to practice law, but are they taught how to manage people? Doctors are taught to practice medicine, but do they know how to run a practice or truly understand bedside manner? Engineers can engineer. Do any of the advanced degree programs teach their students to actually interact with people, interpersonal skills, human relations skills? Quite frankly, it is a setup, an ambush: they have no idea how to manage people, especially people different from them. Masters in Social Work (MSW), Counseling Psychologists, and Psychiatrists might be the closest disciplines that come to understanding this book, using some of these skills and tools every day in their work.

This technique is about you and your feelings, presenting how the actions of a toxic person affect you. How toxic behaviors impact you and your organization or your family. Yes, some people don't like to talk about feelings: get over it. It is the new currency of the evolving, emerging new workplace (post-COVID). I don't have to; I don't want to work for a jerk. Quite frankly, if you ask me, the Great Resignation has been all about people, employees, not wanting to work for a toxic manager or a toxic organization or employer.

> **How do I coach someone when I feel my differences are being held against me?**
>
> **Start with a Positive**
>
> Please stop _____, I feel _____
>   (describe behavior)   (impact of behavior)
> I would prefer _____
>   (new behavior – more appropriate/productive)
>
> **OR**
>
> I feel _____, when you _____
>   (impact of behavior)   (describe behavior)
> I would prefer _____
>   (new behavior – more appropriate/productive)
>
> **OR**
>
> When I see _____, it makes me feel _____
>   (describe behavior)   (impact of behavior on you/group)
> I would prefer _____
>   (new behavior – more appropriate/productive)
>
> **End with a Positive**

This technique is called the "I-Message." Again, you don't attack the person (they will get defensive); separate the person from their behaviors and actions and focus your messaging on their actions and the consequences of these toxic behaviors on you, your team, your organization, your family. I am going to start with the most basic technique and then show you different versions of this technique as we practice and master this technique. This technique and the Stop-Start focus on behaviors and their consequences where you identify the toxic behavior and present an alternative more positive, more acceptable behavior. Stop-Start is more direct, more abrupt so to speak.

First, you start with a positive (+)
When you _____ (describe negative, toxic, destructive, hateful behavior)

I feel _____ (impact on you, impact on your organization, family)

I would prefer _____ (describe alternate more positive behavior, better, more productive, more respectful)

End with a positive (+)

STARTERS AT WORK
"We have a good thing going here."
"You and I work well together."
"I know I can learn a lot from you."
"I value your contributions to our department."

STARTERS AT HOME
"We are family, our children watch us and how we interact."
"We are leaders in this family, we must model appropriate behavior."

NEUTRAL STARTERS
"You and I have been members of this family for x years."
"You and I have known each other a good long time."

1. **When you bad mouth a new hire**
2. **When you criticize a person on our team behind their back**
3. **When you spread rumors and hearsay about a new member in our family**
4. **When you make racist, sexist and gay-bashing remarks and you say "I was just kidding"**
5. **When you have a meeting before or after my meeting without me**
6. **When you don't protect your younger siblings from bullies in your school**

1. I feel you are setting this person up for failure
2. I feel you are trying to undermine their efficacy
3. I feel your comments are not family-like, not loving, and definitely not positive or adding value
4. I feel your comments are hateful, hurtful, not work-related and definitely not funny
5. I feel you are undermining my authority, my role, my team
6. I feel like you are not being a good big brother/big sister

1. I would prefer that you suspend judgment and gossip and focus on your own work
2. I would prefer you give any constructive feedback directly to the person you are talking about
3. I would prefer you give all new family members a chance
4. I would prefer you say positive things about colleagues and team members or say nothing at all
5. I would prefer there be no other meetings before or after my meetings and please share what you are saying in those meetings in my meeting
6. I would prefer you protect your younger siblings

I say this because you are an up and comer.

I say this because you are a star and I want you to continue to succeed.

At Work

You are one of our top contributors on this team. (+)

When all you do is complain and criticize any new project or new initiative or change in policy,

I feel your negativity is setting up these new initiatives for failure.

I would prefer you either say positive, supportive things or nothing at all.

I know you can stay focused on the work at hand. (+)
You are a valued, veteran member of this department. (+)
Your comments have great weight and influence here. (+)
When you criticize a new leader and suggest you don't trust them when you have never met this person before,

I feel like you are trying to influence others, including me, to join you on your negative, hateful crusade.

I would prefer you keep those negative, toxic comments to yourself.

I know we can work better together, stay focused on our greatest challenges, and succeed.

<u>At Home (constructive)</u>
I am so excited about who you are growing up to be. (+)
My job is to prepare you for the real world. (neutral fact)
When you can't keep your room neat or clean,

I feel like you don't deserve an allowance or you are going to make living with your roommate challenging at college.

I would prefer you do the basic chores we ask of you.

<u>Praising at home</u> (slight tweak on technique, not just for constructive use, can be used for praise)
You know I am your biggest fan. (+)
When you keep your room clean, neat,
I feel like you deserve that Xbox you are requesting.
When you do your homework, seek out tutoring (not a weakness to ask for help),

I feel like you are giving this your best effort (all I can ask).

When you tell us when you will be home tonight by a certain time and you honor that time,

I feel like we can really trust you.

I am very proud of you! (+)

Praising at Work

You are really standing out with your recent hard work.

When you come in early, stay late, ask others if they need help before you leave for home,

I feel you are one of the best examples of how to be successful here.

Keep up the good work!

Speaking to a whole group of people at the same time (not singling anyone out)

Look, I know we can all succeed when we work together.(+)

When I see people interrupting each other in a meeting, talking over each other, cutting each other off in midsentence, when men do this to women especially,

I feel this is not professional, not respectful, and counterproductive. It could be harassment.

I would prefer we remember our code of conduct, core values, meeting norms and be nothing less than professional with each other, collegial.

I am addressing all of you at the same time because this team will either succeed or fail together. (fact, neutral)

Now this is a more comprehensive, all-encompassing technique. With both the Stop-Start and I-message techniques, you present the toxic or inappropriate behavior first, and you always present the more positive, more respectful alternative behavior next. You leave nothing to imagination.

In the interviews, people told me their organizations have no training for dealing with these kinds of toxic issues and behaviors. People don't know how to deal with toxic behaviors, don't learn it in school, and their employers don't provide the training. Toxic behaviors live in a vacuum of naive, unskilled targets and victims. Now for some relevant research to drive my points home here.

I have to go back to Professor Porath, Associate Professor at Georgetown University. A November 9, 2022, article in the *Harvard Business Review* presented results of a new survey she conducted in August 2022, "to further track incivility trends and glean more insight into what's happening on the front lines of business and society today." Porath states that "regardless of how individuals define incivility, they're reporting more of it—and have been for a while now." And "In 2005, nearly half of the workers I surveyed across the glove said they were treated rudely at work at least once a month. In 2011, it was up to 55 percent, and by 2016 it had climbed to 62 percent."[1]

For her new survey, she gathered data from more than 2000 people in more than 25 industries in various roles across the globe. They included both frontline employees and people who had observed them at work. Seventy-six percent of respondents said they "experience incivility at least once a month," she reported. In addition, she wrote, 78 percent said they "witness incivility at work at least once a month, and 70 percent witness it at least two to three times a month"; 78 percent "believe that bad behavior from customers toward employees is more common than it was five years ago"; and "66 percent believe bad behavior from customers toward other customers is more common than it was five years ago." These 2022 numbers, she noted, "have risen steadily and sharply" since a 2012 survey she did.[2]

Stress and anxiety way up, add COVID to the mix with social media accelerating the spread of all this toxicity and negativity in an election year? No wonder so many tell me this book is timely for our volatile political times. What a diabolical cocktail of contributing factors coming together. Again, I did not want to put out a book that was just focused on the workplace. You will see I alternate chapters between workplace and the rest of your life.

How about people behaving badly in sporting events (all over social media, at our children's events), at car dealerships (salespeople), or on airplanes? The next chapter and later chapters are dedicated to these "special moments" to never be forgotten. I want to show you how I deal with these situations because it is not as much about the toxic behaviors as it is about how we respond to them, not react. How we resolve the human relations conflict, how we solve the interpersonal problems.

CHAPTER 7.

FROM BYSTANDER TO UPSTANDER—IN ALL ASPECTS OF YOUR LIFE, SPORTS FOR STARTERS

Most of us have been to sporting events for our kids, and too many of us have witnessed that one particular out-of-control parent, or God help us, more than one parent getting into it, egging each other on and nearly coming to blows. Of course, their spouses are nowhere to be found. I get it, their spouses are just exhausted (and embarrassed, of course). This is why we need more people skilled up, with commitment and confidence, to engage these toxic parents. We need more peacemakers.

This story is very close to my heart because I did not have the support of certain people as I challenged the toxic parent. Often, many of us don't, yet we feel like we have to say or do something. Social media is littered with these horrible videos, whole groups of parents getting in a brawl.

So, let's start with one of the most difficult toxic sporting situations I have ever had to deal with!

EIGHTH GRADE GIRLS ARE PLAYING BASKETBALL, AND YOU ARE CURSING?

I had been away for nearly two weeks on business travel to Japan, Guam, and Hawaii training for the United States Navy, Bureau of Medicine. My client was the Surgeon General of the US Navy. He sent me to train at every Naval Base Clinic or Hospital in the whole world except Diego Garcia. This was the longest trip I had been away from my family, and my phone blew up with text messages as I landed at Washington Dulles Airport.

My daughter's eighth grade basketball season had started and I had missed a couple of games. I don't like to miss these games because although our team was not tall, they were athletic as hell and wore down the other teams with their tenacious and committed play. They were in tremendous shape (unlike their parents). The prior season they had gone undefeated and won the league championship. Two of the fathers were reaching out to me urgently via text and email.

"Where have you been? We missed you at the first few games. We need to talk to you before the next game."

I was like, *This is odd, what's up?*

A particular dad, let's call him Jon, was quite toxic at the first two games. He would yell a lot, curse, rant, and pace back and forth. He would yell at the referees (curse, scream, "Get your head out of your...") at our coach and, yes, his daughter was very good. Oh, take her out and he would lose his mind. But what was also troubling was none of the parents were even looking back at him with a stare or possibly an ugly face. The parents of the opposing team were definitely looking over at this toxic parent who was just yelling the whole time.

I'd known this father for years from other teams where our daughters played together. Jon was infamous for his toxicity. The problem? None of the other parents on our team would say anything; they were conflict avoiders, conflict averse, and I think they feared confrontation. I think Jon interpreted their silence as tacit support or agreement with his toxic antics.

So, I huddled with two concerned dads over the telephone. They told me that he was going to new toxic heights, and the referees were turning on our girls. They needed my help.

"My help?" I asked. "Wait, have none of you or the other parents said or done anything?"

"There have been concerned, heated conversations out in the parking lot among many of the parents after the games, but no one has said anything directly to Jon. We were hoping you might say something."

"Me?"

"Mauricio, we know what you do for a living, and we suspect you could help. Can we meet before the next game in the parking lot and come up with a game plan for Jon?"

I agreed. At the next game, Kelly and I arrived early, and I huddled with a bunch of the dads on the team.

"He sits right up there, top right corner of the bleachers. I will sit here next to him, you next to me, and the other dad will sit in front of him." We will have him boxed in, so to speak. Kelly will sit next to me, of course.

The starting whistle blew, and sure enough Jon started pacing back and forth. I kept looking over at him. Eventually he started yelling, screaming, and cursing. You know the drill. I was about to stand up, turn, and say something but, Kelly put her arm on my shoulder,

"Please don't say anything, don't get involved."

Kelly does not like me confronting issues at certain times; she feels it embarrasses her and our family. She would rather I just watch and say nothing. Sorry, I can't do that. If I did nothing, I would lament for days, "Why didn't I get involved, why didn't I say something?" Also, this was the first game we had made it to this season, and neither of us knew how bad it was until we saw it, experienced it.

I looked at Kelly. "I was put on the planet for these special moments."

I shrugged her off, stood up, and turned toward the center of the toxic tornado.

"Jon, Jon, Jon, these are eighth graders, girls. Man, are you okay? We're supposed to role model appropriate behavior. This is not an NBA game; have you been drinking beers?"

As I have witnessed in the past and feared, the only parents looking back at him were the parents of the girls from the opposing team. Oh, have I mentioned this is a Catholic league?

Jon turned to me, snarled, and looked like he was getting ready to throw a punch. Thank God the basketball dad between us, who is a bigger guy, stood up and intervened. Jon sat down, grumbling under his breath. Things calmed down right before the first half. Jon and I were exchanging evil looks and stares, but now a couple of the other dads were looking back to make sure a fight did not ensue.

Elise, my daughter on the team, came up the bleachers at half. "Dad, that was so embarrassing!"

"Wait, embarrassing? Me? I was just standing up to this bully Jon."

Kelly chimed in with, "You see, I told you so! So embarrassing."

Before this animated, heated conversation continued, a woman came up to me (I was sitting on the aisle) behind Elise. "Are you Mr. Velásquez?" she asked.

"Why yes. How can I help you?" I'd never seen her before. She was nicely dressed and a little older.

"I am the commissioner of the league, and I wanted to come and personally thank you." Now I am looking at Elise and Kelly, they are startled by this new development.

"I'm sorry, what?" I wanted her to be very clear here, and I knew Kelly and Elise were listening attentively.

"Mr. Velásquez, we need more parents like you in the stands. Do you know how many of these characters I get in our games, and I cannot be at all the games. I was out in the parking lot leaving at the end of the last game when a parent from your game came out and grabbed me and told me there was something developing in the stands. I just want to shake your hand and thank you and tell you to please keep up the good work." As she finished talking, she looked over at Jon and then we all looked over at him.

Jon was being escorted out of the gym by two police officers, one hand on each shoulder. You could tell Jon was part agitated, part embarrassed. I could not be happier. With a huge smile, I looked at Kelly and Elise.

"What's happening?"

"Oh, I called the police to escort him out of the gym. I banned him from the league. You won't see him anymore this season. Thanks again, Mr. Velásquez."

"Oh, please call me Mauricio and can I call you Commish?" Remember that show? I loved that show. As I laughed, you could tell she knew the show I was referencing.

Commish walked back down the bleachers, and I immediately turned to Kelly and Elise. This has happened so many times where I did not always have the support of parties present, especially those averse to conflict and confrontation.

"So, you were embarrassed by me? I am embarrassed by the two of you. Elise, what have I always said to you about bullies in school? Say something, don't be quiet on the sidelines. Your friends being bullied will always remember you stood up for them. We have to get off the sideline and get involved, go from bystander to upstander, or nothing changes, and we all suffer silently."

Kelly looked confused, uncertain. "Okay, maybe..."

"Maybe? There is no maybe in dealing with bullies and their toxic behaviors. You are either a part of the problem, saying and doing nothing and quietly supporting them, or you are a part of the solution and say something, do something."

I really tire of conflict avoiders trying to stop conflict confronters from saying something, doing something. Support that bystander who is now an upstander in your family or workplace. Get in the game, get in the action, or don't complain about it later.

I was curious what research may be out there to support this story.

From the All Pro Dad website's blog "Confronting Crazy Sports Parents," author BJ Foster states that "A majority of kids polled said they quit playing sports because it ceased to be fun due to parental pressure."[1]

Or if you research a little more, it was a 2016 *Washington Post* article entitled "Why 70 Percent of Kids Quit Sports by Age 13" that highlighted a poll from the National Alliance for Youth Sports, which sounded the alarm: "around 70 percent of kids in the United States stop playing organized sports by the age of 13 because 'it's just not fun anymore.'"[2]

My understanding is this player stopped playing basketball (and she was real good, a rising star, probably the best on the team), and I attribute this to her father's toxic antics.

What follows is a story of transformation; a person I know who used to be an avoider rises up like a Phoenix to be a confronter. From bystander to upstander (I know I say this a lot, but it is one of the themes in this book).

Journal: I know you have been here before, or you know someone who has. What did you do? Nothing? Say something? Leave?

SPEAK NOW OR FOREVER HOLD YOUR PEACE!

Kelly uttered that phrase I was dreading.

"We need a van," she said.

We had a Volvo station wagon at the time, but baby number three was on the way and you could not put three car seats in the back row of the wagon, so we needed a bigger car with a third row of seats for the third car seat. I dreaded this day would come. For me, getting a van meant we were throwing in the towel, getting old and stuff. Also, my station wagon was a Volvo T-5, turbo-charged, rocket, and I loved that car. Slate gray, with Z-rated tires.

Kelly was persuasive. I mean, she was right; we needed a bigger kid carrier.

"Okay, let's go get one," I agreed.

Kelly is a very thorough buyer; she had done her research, and she knew exactly what she wanted. A Honda

Odyssey, top of the line; the only thing she did not want was the built in vacuum cleaner (crazy expensive).

We walked into the Honda dealership and a salesperson came right up to us. "Can I help?" he asked, looking directly at me.

"Oh, Kelly, my wife here is looking for a new van."

He briefly looked at her and then back at me. "So what features are you looking for? How much do you want to spend? Color preference?" And on and on.

"Listen, please stop looking at me, talking directly or only to me. Kelly here is the buyer. Actually, she pays all our bills. I am just the driver, the chauffeur. Consider me a cardboard cutout." I smiled and laughed.

Kelly, meanwhile, was not smiling at this point. I knew why; this guy was ignoring her, diminishing her. Kelly began to tell him everything she wanted: color, leather, CD changer in trunk, TV/video for kids, refrigerator, storage, etc.

The salesman looked at Kelly and said, "Wow, honey, you are full of piss and vinegar, aren't you? You really know what you want, huh?"

I looked at him, stunned with what he was saying and how he was saying it. I mean all wrapped in one exchange, one attack really: sexist, misogynist, condescending.

I looked at him and said quickly, "Please just go get the van Kelly wants so we can take it for a test drive."

He was not picking up on the fact that my wife was getting angrier and angrier, barely looking at him but starting to look at me. As he went to get the van, I tried to calm Kelly down. I could see proverbial steam coming out her ears.

The salesman pulled the van around and grabbed me by the arm. He put me in the driver's seat. Then, he escorted

Kelly to the passenger seat, shut the door, flipped down the sun visor, turned on the light, and said to Kelly, "For your makeup!"

Kelly erupted. "That's it. We are out of here! This guy does not get one nickel from us." She looked directly at me. "Let's go!"

"Yes, Kelly." We exited the van and headed to the front exit, the front major doors.

Meanwhile the salesman is trailing us. "Hey, what did I do? What did I say?"

In our path to our car parked out front was somebody we had not met before. I suspect he is the sales manager, and he stopped us at the door, blocking us really.

"I feel like we are about to lose a sale?" the manager asked.

"You are very perceptive. Now please step aside." Kelly was silent, just ready to boil over. If she were a volcano, we were in full getting-ready-to-erupt mode.

"Please, tell me what happened," the manager pleaded. "How can I make amends?" Our actual salesman was just standing there watching, quietly, as his boss had taken over.

I looked at Kelly. "Okay, he wants to know what happened. Speak now, or forever hold your peace."

You see, what will happen is Kelly will say nothing but then yell at me all the way home. This was that moment. You can speak up, speak your mind, or leave and regret later not having said anything. As a trainer, coach, I could see a teachable moment for the sales manager and his dealership. They are sexists and don't know it, or worse, don't care. But their actions have consequences. They are about to lose a boatload of money.

Kelly looked the manager right in the eye with an intensity and said, "Okay, I came here to give you cash (always start with a positive to get their attention). When your salesperson here never looked at me, (she looked straight at him for a moment, more time than he ever gave her), never addressed me the way he addressed my husband, I felt unimportant. If my husband is Mr. Velásquez, I am Mrs. Velásquez, not sweetie, honey, sugar, darlin', and the rest of that nonsense."

Kelly was now on a roll. "You look at me, talk to me, especially after my husband explicitly told you I am the customer (all behavioral). Since you treated me so poorly, I prefer to take my business elsewhere. Oh, and when we purchase this van from another dealership, and we will today, they will get all of my service business, and I will tell everyone I know what a sexist shit show you are running here. We are out of here! By the way, I know Honda vans are the best, and you are selling the best."

I watched Kelly "go off" with this deep sense of admiration. Kelly had transformed from an avoider to a confronter, and she stood up for herself in such a way; I could not be prouder. Oh, and I am sure when we walked out, the manager and the salesperson who helped us either said to themselves "What a bitch" or "We just lost $45,000." Can you guess which sentiment gets you nowhere and which sentiment moves people to change? (Pissed off customers don't accept toxic treatment, and we tell everyone.)

Sidenote: What percentage of cars and vans and trucks are purchased by women or the buying decision is heavily influenced by women? "Sixty-two percent of all new cars and trucks sold in the US are bought by women," according to research from Cars.com, which also found that women "influence more than 85 percent of all car and truck purchases."[3]

In our house, Kelly makes 100 percent of the buying decisions. Oh, and go check out where you find the car advertisements in the newspaper—the sports section. I wonder how many women look at the sports section at all. Why are people buying cars on the internet? To skip this nightmare experience. And go to a car show (I am a car guy). Who is standing next to the new cars? Beautiful scantily clad women. "Where are the hunks, the beef cakes?" Kelly asks.

We have to stop avoiding the conflict and start embracing it, or toxic people are going to walk all over us. Bullies thrive in an environment of a bunch of avoiders. I call it "feeding the monster"; we feed the monster with our inaction.

I know you have been here or know someone who has. Now this story was a transformative experience for Kelly. As she gets older, I see Kelly putting up with less and less shit.

There are moments when I will go it alone. When no one is going to say something, and I just have to blurt something out because the silence is deafening and I can't live with myself staying on the sidelines. One of these moments was on a packed flight to Florida.

SOMEBODY SHUT THAT KID UP!

You know I fly a lot, over 1.5 million miles in my career, and I find too many travelers are so wound up and nerves can be raw. So, I was on a flight to Florida and there was a small child behind me. Her mom looks frazzled, and the cute daughter was active, squirming, cranky, kicking, and grabbing the back of my seat. Now I don't say anything because I had small children of my own at the time and I got it; it happens to the best of us. Empathy is so important, and actually showing support, conveying that support, is critical. I was smiling at mom and daughter as I sat down in my seat.

The cutie pie reaches through the seats and touches my head, my hair. I turn and mom looks mortified. "I am so sorry," she says.

I make eye contact, smile, and say, "All good, no worries, I understand. I have kids of my own. She is really cute."

Mom looks tired, like she is at end of her patience. I actually gave the little traveler something I had, a trinket, to distract the daughter. This worked for a period of time.

A little while later, someone else on this flight just ahead of me on the airplane speaks out rather loudly, but anonymously, "Can someone please shut that kid up!" She said it loudly but not directly at anyone. We were all pretty sure who she was talking about, but I knew the mom and her daughter behind me heard the comment. I looked back.

Now I had to say something.

"Look," I said, "if you do not want to be on a flight with small children, then don't fly to Orlando, Florida, right? Earplugs or headphones do the trick." I looked back at the mom with her daughter and smile, and she mouthed to me "Thank you." I turned to the person traveling with me. He looked somewhat surprised, and I said to him, "Amateurs."

I put on my headphones and fell into a wonderful slumber. Never heard from that toxic traveler again. Sometimes you have to stick up for someone else who might not feel they can; they might be embarrassed. We are all in this together. Together we must all stand for civility, dignity, respect.

Journal: Have you ever stood up for someone else, almost anonymously? It can be fun.

CONFLICT IS NOT BAD! NOT TO BE AVOIDED. WE MUST DEAL WITH IT—HEAD-ON

All too often you read about or see a news story where something horrible happened and certain parties saw it coming but did nothing. There were signs that went ignored. With nearly every high school shooting or workplace shooting, certain people, certain parties knew something prior to the conflict eruption and did nothing. This just kills me inside. Personally, I just can't fathom having such knowledge and just sitting on it. And the guilt knowing after the horrible event that you could have said or done something earlier would just eat me alive.

Look, ignoring conflict, ignoring toxic behaviors, does not make them go away. I hear this all of the time: "Oh, I just thought if I looked the other way, swept the issues under the rug, denied their existence, the pattern of toxic behaviors and related issues would resolve themselves, would just go away."

What, are you kidding me? Are you high or something? No, definitely not. They fester. What was once a brush fire, easy to manage, especially if you caught it right at the early stages of conflict, of toxicity, has now become a ten-alarm forest fire engulfing anyone and everyone in its path.

Long-term unresolved, unaddressed conflict, toxicity (pattern of hateful, awful, not civil behaviors) is at the root of so many explosions of toxicity in our society, in our world for that matter. Just turn on the TV and you hear the commentators: "Oh, people saw this coming!"

So why didn't anyone say or do anything before the fact? Why didn't someone, anyone, not try to head this off at the pass?

So many just watch and later lament, "I should have said or done something." What an empty thought—a waste of time really.

Tragic really. Maybe they wanted to say something but were either fearful of saying something or just did not know how.

CHANGE THE NARRATIVE

First, we have to reorient our attitude, our perception of how we see conflict and toxic behaviors. We have to change the narrative. Put a different set of lenses on our perceptual eyes. Conflict is not bad or something to ignore or avoid. We have to rethink our approach. We cannot be afraid to confront the toxic behaviors: if we don't, if no one does, the toxicity continues and spreads.

I think conflict and toxic behaviors are a test. Our parenting, leadership, managerial, supervisory abilities are being tested. We pass the test, endure and resolve the conflict, and it will make us stronger.

Toxic behaviors are an opportunity to grow. I always said to Kelly, "Okay, your family does not like me, and my family does not like you (at first). This is a test. It will make us stronger if we deal with it head-on together."

LEARN WHAT TO DO

Second, most people do not know how to address toxic behaviors. They lack the skill or knowledge, and knowledge is the application or practice of using a particular skill to address an emerging toxic situation.

Or worse, people just don't want to get involved. Or even worse, some people just don't care. If the whole world does not care about dealing with toxic behaviors, this lack of civility, this lack of decency, then we are all going down together. The end of civilization if you ask me.

In the last couple of years, if you observe current events, we are in a watershed moment. A tipping point. Divisiveness, toxic manipulation, a call to violent arms, and so many people are witnessing this, watching from proverbial sidelines and saying nothing, doing nothing. This lack of civility, decency, and respect for others, especially those different from the toxic party, cannot become the new normal. You are called a snowflake if you believe in decency, civility, in resolving conflict, solving problems. When did being civil and decent become a weakness?

A certain political leader I know, we all know, really brought being a jerk back to mainstream. This "it is cool to fight, to attack, to be the smash mouth, to denigrate, personally insult others" camp of people is a blight on my commitment to civility, decency, and respect for all. These folks with this cockiness, this nuke civility for morbid orientation and attitude, was a big motivator behind me writing this book. Every day, so many people present in and around all this hate, this toxicity, privy to the toxic behaviors, and no one calls it out, no one says anything. Just disgusting if you ask me. Where have all the peacemakers gone?

"I swore never to be silent whenever and wherever human beings endure suffering and humiliation. We must always take sides." —Elie Wiesel

So again, we need skills, tools, methods, approaches to tackle the toxic behaviors in all aspects of our life. What if you only tackled toxicity in part of your life but it thrived in other parts of your life? You would not be whole. You would be living a lie. Well here comes another technique, simple but powerful. And easy to use.

You are being toxic – you may not be aware, unintentional

THE "T"

Toxic behaviors create interpersonal conflict. If you don't respond to the conflict, you internalize the impact of the toxic behaviors and it will eat at you, like a cancer. You are present, you watch someone else suffer, you don't say or do anything, and the target of the toxicity interprets your silence as tacit support, agreement. Now, many people say or do nothing until they have to do something or lose their mind, lose control, and possibly quit instead of speaking their piece.

I have clients who really believe in this technique. Participants in my workshops have said, "Oh, I use this technique all the time." It is especially powerful because it is nonverbal. I use this technique at home and at work, but it is particularly effective on a Zoom or virtual call where we can all see each other. It's a formidable technique in, say, large group meetings where you have to communicate nonverbally across the room.

This technique was forged in the fires of my personal, family life. Let's say you have a particularly toxic family member or coworker who feels very comfortable around you to be terrible, horrible, in front of other people. They might actually wear this toxicity like a badge of honor. They might also warn you ahead of time: "Oh, I am in a terrible mood."

So, at home there is this one person who tends to be "very dramatic," and they are often in denial that they are being so negative, so toxic. This person is not self-aware. They will complain about anything and everything, how unhappy they are, the weather, their neighbors for example. This person is very suspicious of people around them; they don't trust anyone. Some of the toxic comments include...

... "You look fat; have you put on weight?"
... "Your hair...what happened?"
... "You look worn down, tired."
... "Your house looks dirty, not taken care of, etc."
... "Your outfit...is that appropriate for today?"

When this happens again and again, I immediately put up a "T" sign, one hand on top horizontally and the other below vertically.

T for Toxic

T for Too Much Information

T for Time Out

It is a family event that comes to mind. The toxic person in question does not like when I do this, and she will quickly pivot and walk over to my brother or sister looking for an audience, someone to listen to her rant. I will convey the T across the room to my siblings, and they will know "this person is bringing the toxicity; they are on the toxic prowl, looking for listeners."

My brother will put up his "T" (he saw my "T" across the room) before this person actually gets to him. My sister will also put up the "T" before actual engagement. All three of us, with our "T" up, will back this person into a corner of my den (or living room), and the last time we did this (like a spot intervention), I joked, "Back, back, back from where you came" like this person was a vampire and we were all holding up a blessed silver cross (huge fan of vampire movies). We all started laughing, the target of our intervention got it, and we all walked away like it never happened.

This person did not exhibit any more toxicity that night. They were quiet, inwardly focused, and we were all fine with that. The calm after the storm can be nice; the individual who has been called out hopefully gets quiet, introspective, and really starts to question their actions and, more important, start to consider the consequences of their actions.

It takes planning, courage, tact, and most importantly skill to *Tackle Toxicity*. First thing we have to do is separate the person from their toxic behaviors and the horrible consequences of said behaviors. As some say in church: love the person, hate the sin. Well guess what? So many of the people who say this have no idea what they are talking about or how to do it. Not to mention...sin?

Earlier in this book, I used the phrase "Toxic Individual or Person" to get your attention, but I want to reiterate that you have to separate the person from their horrible toxic actions. Actions have consequences (I will say this over and over again). If you attack the toxic individual, they get defensive, they will not hear you, they will not listen to you, and they will definitely not change or modify their behaviors, their actions, and you and others will continue to suffer (silently).

In any toxic situation—at work, home, school, church, wherever—always focus on the toxic behaviors, the pattern or pathology of the behaviors, and the consequences of said actions.

The "T" I came up with myself. I mean, we have all seen the "T" used for "Time Out." I put additional meaning on it. I use it at home and at work; it's especially effective in the age of Zoom and virtual meetings: so perfect for the video medium, silent, but very on point. Time out, too much information, toxic: multiple meanings but they all convey "Stop, be aware of what you are saying and doing."

Again, in the interviews, people are clamoring, especially supervisors and managers, just desperate for a skill; they need a tool, a technique to help convey what they are thinking: "Please stop, you are 'over the respectful line.' Stop, don't you know you have gone too far?"

In the next chapter, you will see examples, stories, where the role of the person, their power, amplifies certain toxic dynamics.

Journal: You have to try this very simple technique—it works! Do you have a family member like this?

CHAPTER 8.

CHIEF OF FIRE DEPARTMENT, CHIEF OF TOXICITY

There are times when I have come across a leader so reckless, so out of control, so clueless that I just could not believe what was happening. This story is at the top of my "clueless leaders" list. This chief of a volunteer fire department was also surrounded by cronies, "yes men" who I believe "let him run" because they said nothing about his behavior. So, they hired an outsider to come in and evaluate the situation. The gatekeepers in essence protected their chief and did not inform their board of his toxic antics.

I WAS TOLD YOU WERE A VIP

A board member of a nearby volunteer fire department called me. "Can you come out here and take a look at our fire department? We are facing a lawsuit, and we want your input, your perspective."

I always start with a site visit. "Sure, I'm free in ten days. Please tell the chief I'm coming."

I arrived that day and the chief was waiting for me. He was a pleasant fellow, older, nice, and welcomed me with a kind of hanging-out, guys-chatter, locker-room-banter vibe.

We started in the garage. He showed me their "big equipment" and pointed out their capabilities and how much they cost to purchase. Some seriously expensive hardware. He then said to me, "Let me show you my pride and joy." I was a little surprised because I would think the big trucks would be his pride and joy. When I was little and when my son was little, we were both huge fans of fire trucks and their fire warriors. We headed upstairs.

Chief said, "Now we are headed to the media room, my favorite part of our facility." Connected to that was the sleeping quarters (right off the kitchen and the media room). Before I walked in, I am told all the fire professionals (men and women side by side) sleep in the one room, a barracks-like situation set up with bunk beds.

As I walked in, I was immediately taken aback. Shocked really. I froze for a moment. The walls were plastered with posters, pinups: busty topless or naked women, wall-to-wall. I looked at the chief with my "this is a joke, right?" face.

Chief looked at me. "What do you think? I have some vintage pieces up, right? Also, come over here."

He brought me over to a large piece of furniture near the big-screen TV. He rolled open drawer after drawer of pornography.

"I have Betamax, VHS, DVD, the whole enchilada."

I was thinking, *Am I being punked? Is this a joke?* But no, he was completely serious. Chief was smiling but asking me for my reaction, looking at my facial expression for what I thought of his media room. He was looking for affirmation, confirmation, appreciation really, for his lifelong passion.

"We have movie night every Friday night." He implies that his porn collection is the mainstay of their Friday night programming. He asks again, "What do you think?"

"I am speechless, Chief. Sorry, but what were you told about me before I came today?"

"I was told you were a VIP."

"Chief, if I were a reporter, a journalist, a politician, what would you be doing differently with my tour?"

"Oh, if you were a reporter, a journalist, a political leader, I would take everything down from the walls, and I would never show you my collection of videos, movies. Then after you left, I would put everything back up."

"Wow, at least you are being candid with me."

"Wait, hold on a second. What?"

"Chief, I am an investigator, an expert witness, and the harassment consultant hired by your board to conduct an investigation given the lawsuit this department is facing."

A look of fresh concern came over his face as I pulled out my mobile phone and started taking pictures and videos of the walls of the room and the video collection.

"What are you doing? What is happening here? Why are you taking pictures and video?"

"Chief, do you know what these pictures and videos represent in the courtroom? I fear you also sent out emails and flyers about Friday night porn night. All of these items are called *evidence*." I raised my voice for emphasis. "And I suspect the two plaintiffs suing you, the department, and the union already have these pictures and videos and will be ready to present at trial. Chief, you don't think the two women on your staff felt uncomfortable about your porn night? I mean, you made everyone come and discouraged nonparticipation. How did the women feel during the actual watching of the videos? Were comments made? I can't imagine a jury not empathizing with, not feeling for, the two plaintiffs."

The two plaintiffs sued and bankrupted their union because the union did not back them or support them and the volunteer fire department and their board of course were completely in the dark. The board had no idea what was happening, and they had to pay out a huge settlement, bankrupting the volunteer fire department (often run on a very thin budget). In legal terms, the chief was creating a hostile work environment and also keeping it from the board.

I sent the photos and videos to the board and the chief was abruptly fired (forget his retirement monies, he lost all of it). What really concerned me the most though, was that none of the other firefighters ever felt this media room, the porn night, the emails, the flyers, and all the banter around it was inappropriate. Not one of them complained? Not one of them went directly to the board?

My contact on the board asked me, "Who might be the next leader in this department?"

I replied, "Well, since none complained, since not one firefighter came to the board, sent a note, not even an email, I think this disqualifies all from being leadership potential." The board contact agreed. They had to go outside the organization to find a new chief.

Journal: Some folks just don't get it, but they also thrive when those around them don't call them out. Have you come across this kind of situation? What did you do?

WHITE POWER

I was asked to consult on a situation with a state government employee whose car had a fresh new "white power" sticker on his bumper. His colleagues were a little concerned about some of his recent comments regarding the white race and inferior races, and his emails were getting stranger and stranger as current events agitated him.

Upon meeting him, I noticed the tattoo peering out on one of his arms right below the sleeve. It was a swastika. I was told the tattoo was often more visible. His office had some, shall we say, very interesting literature, and white national symbols visible to anyone who would walk by his cubicle. He was outspoken at times about current events that dealt with race.

He would often mention "freedom of speech" arguments if anyone even appeared uncomfortable with him and his beliefs. What he and so many don't understand is that with freedom of speech comes consequences. Your free speech cannot impinge on or restrict someone else's right to exist. But you see, if he kept his toxic comments and beliefs to himself that was one thing. I mean, you can't be held accountable for your thoughts, right? He was going too far in his conversations and his emails with his colleagues. He had crossed lines of respect and dignity for all.

So this employee and I had a quick coaching session, a meeting of sorts. He was not keen on our time together. Intuitively, he knew he was making some of his colleagues uncomfortable. He works for the taxpayers, his constituents so to speak, and they were complaining as they entered the building. In our coaching session, I presented a couple of concepts.

"Hey, this is a free country right," he said. "I mean, freedom of speech, right?"

"With *freedom of speech* comes *consequences, responsibility*. You can decide to say something, anything, and you will be held to account for the consequences of said speech. Yes, we live in a great country." He did not deny what he said. He could not deny the emails he had sent out.

"I think some folks around here have a thin skin, honestly. They're a little too sensitive for my tastes."

"When you say something, you cannot choose or decide how your speech is heard, received, or how it lands on others. You cannot tell other people how to feel. 'I did not mean to offend' is not relevant or pertinent because no one can read your mind." I figured that was the next thing he was going to say.

"No one knows your intent. What we know is what you said."

"You cannot selectively choose whose speech is hateful or threatening. It is or it is not. Oh, and don't say 'It depends.' That is not true."

I was trying to anticipate his next salvo of defensive gibberish. It is called the "Reasonable Person Standard" in the courtroom. Would a "reasonable person find such conduct hateful or threatening?"

He shared a common refrain. "Don't you think some people are making a mountain out of a molehill?" I have always thought this was an interesting phrase.

Again, a common way to minimize responsibility for your own actions is to be blame the target: "Don't be so sensitive." *You cannot tell other people how to feel.* In my executive coaching work, every day these dynamics, lies really, reflect a lack of emotional intelligence. Actually, these folks are emotionally illiterate or completely self-unaware (narcissistic?).

He would not agree with me; he did not see the point of any of my coaching and feedback. I closed with pointing out that none of his racist comments were work-related, agency or mission related, and quite frankly did not fall in the purview of his job. He did not care; he said as much.

He was shocked that he was let go. I reminded him as he was being escorted out by local law enforcement that this is an at-will state. There is a lot of wiggle room for letting someone go. Meaning employers may legally fire an employee at any time, for any reason, without cause, although in this instance there was plenty of cause.

"Freedom of speech, this is a violation of my rights" he babbled as he was being taken away. Hate speech, toxic speech, and all the related hateful emails I think warrant this kind of consequence.

I closed with, "You cannot use one part of the Constitution to violate another part of the Constitution."

I was surprised at how upset I was at this person for thinking he could impose his hatred on others, spread his hate, and then be so nonchalant about the consequences. I also think the lack of regret, the lack of empathy, the lack of understanding how he hurts people and actually scares people was troubling to me.

Journal: I hope you have not met one of these scary type bullies. Have you? What did you do? So many people said nothing for a long time out of fear he might get violent in this last story.

ARE YOU A PROFESSIONAL OR AN AMATEUR

A simple technique I use at times is to remind people of the distinction between being a professional or being an amateur. "Professionals get the job done, amateurs make excuses." And I say it with gusto. I remind the person getting feedback from me that the last time I checked, they were a professional, being paid to be here, "so step up and act like a professional." Sometimes you have to be firm.

I worked in restaurants for years, earning my way through college, and I often use this technique in a restaurant.

"Hey, I love this place, your food. Were you stiffed by the previous customer? Because I am feeling this is Amateur Hour. We have not seen you for over thirty minutes. Look, professionals get this done and amateurs make excuses. I tip very well for good to great service. Rise up, partner." All said with a smile. Usually the response is an explanation or an excuse, but they do respond with better service.

Interviews conducted for this book revealed that toxic people can be very bold, very in your face, aggressive at times. Interviews were also very insightful when we talked about preparing to meet with a toxic person. Script what you are going to say prior to the pending meeting. Anticipate, ready yourself, prepare for the toxic behaviors to come at you. Don't get rattled, don't let them see you sweat. Have a set of ground rules posted on the wall, rules of engagement or code of conduct—call them what you want. You need rules because toxic people thrive in an environment of no rules or accountability.

Especially with the super angry, super manipulative toxic person, always look for the toxic mentor, the higher up who has role modeled the toxic behaviors and created an environment for these toxic behaviors to thrive and fester.

In the next chapter, I present what happens when these toxic individuals are embedded in some of society's most powerful and life-influencing industries like real estate.

CHAPTER 9.

LIVING THE AMERICAN DREAM—SOME TOXIC FOLKS TRY TO RUIN IT

There are certain industries that play a powerful role and have great influence over our lives. In a previous chapter, we discussed my favorite car dealership story. In this one, we will talk about the real estate industry. I was taken aback when we experienced these toxic moments. I was also dismayed at how quickly I felt so agitated. I tried not to show it, instead trying to stay calm, cool, and collected in all these situations.

As the son of immigrants, my family lived in an apartment, then moved to a smaller home, and finally a powder blue split-level house in McLean, Virginia. I always had a dream of a house with a garage. When my parents came to visit me in my new home for the first time, I noticed them standing out front, just staring at our house. I came out to greet them.

"What are you doing out here?"

My mother and father said, "You have a garage! You are the first in our family to have a garage."

My father had commented before that he was not sure how successful I was, starting my own company and all that. Now he said, "I guess you are doing okay, maybe better than I thought."

"Thanks," I said, "I think." They were surprised at my success? Was that a compliment? I didn't know. "Great, can we go inside now?"

I had always wondered what kind of house I would purchase and make a home. Marrying Kelly, we were getting closer to my dream being fulfilled. We were two successful professionals. What follows are our early real estate adventures; I am sure many can relate. I also fear the real estate industry is not progressing or changing fast enough for the better.

CAN I HELP YOU? I'M THE AGENT ON DUTY

Kelly and I got married later in life. When Kelly and I met, I lived on *The Big Mamou*, a thirty-six-foot houseboat docked at Harborview Marina and Yacht Club in downtown, Baltimore, Maryland. I lived on my boat for five years, "a live aboard" as I was called. My slip fee was $300 per month and my boat payment was $220 per month (the good old days). My housing costs were ridiculously low and manageable. No grass to cut, no taxes to pay. I started my firm, Diversity Training Group, on my boat. It was low overhead, allowing me to save lots of money for sure. Life was good.

When Kelly and I married, she lived in a 1.5 bedroom, 1.5 bath apartment in Federal Hill, the top half of a row house. Kelly was a practicing speech pathologist, doing very well for herself, and she had also saved up money. I would travel a lot, and while I was traveling Kelly would go out and about on a mission to find our first home. No, we did not have to get another apartment together or buy a townhouse first; we were going straight to our dream house (hopefully).

We met in Baltimore, but Kelly is from Charlottesville, Virginia, and I was raised in Arlington and primarily McLean, Virginia. We settled on finding our first home somewhere in Northern Virginia. I had one stipulation: it had to be near an airport since I flew a lot for work.

As would any person who is not from Northern Virginia, Kelly gets lost one day in one of her real estate hunting runs. She pulls into a local real estate office, walked in, and asked for help.

The agent on duty said, "Please fill out this paperwork, and we'll be off. I'll drive and show you around."

"He seemed nice at first," Kelly told me later. Kelly climbed into his real estate cruiser, a big car, just hovering above the ground, and he started showing her all around Herndon, Virginia (right next to Washington, Dulles Airport). When I grew up in McLean, Herndon was "in the sticks" out by that airport in the middle of nowhere.

Kelly was asking many questions. "Where are the schools, show me the grocery stores, nearest parks, etc." There was a particular part of Herndon that our real estate agent kept skipping, driving by, and not mentioning.

Eventually Kelly asked, "Hey, how about this part of Herndon? It looks nice and seems close to everything."

The real estate agent said, "Oh, no, you don't want to live in this part of town. It's primarily a Hispanic, Latino area; they live like twenty to a house, crap all over the front yard, high crime, gangs, no, no, dangerous, you don't want to see that part of town."

"Pull over for a minute," Kelly said in a stern, not-so-friendly voice. She repeated what he just said back to him. Kelly asked, "Did you even look at the paperwork I filled out?"

He pulled out the paperwork on a clipboard in the side pocket of his car door. He looked at Kelly. "Oh, I had no idea."

"Yes, I am Kelly Velásquez (using her excellent Spanish accent; she can sound better than my immigrant parents when she tries). "My husband is Mauricio Velásquez." Kelly raised her voice to emphasize our last name.

"Oh, I had no idea, I did not mean to..."

Kelly interrupted him, "We are headed back to your office now, and I want to talk to your boss!"

What he was doing is illegal. What he was saying and doing, not showing Kelly a particular neighborhood because she is White and that neighborhood is predominately Latino, is a blatant violation of the Fair Housing Standards Act.[1] Know what this is called? Herding.

You go to the bank and ask for a mortgage for a house in "that neighborhood" and they deny you because of the location of said neighborhood: that is redlining. Redlining created or contributed to the formation of "all blank" neighborhoods. You think this happens naturally? It is institutional and toxic.

We definitely did not give this real estate office our business. We decided to do our own research and go looking on our own. I had some time off the road, and we went hunting. I even prequalified our eligibility for our mortgage, and we knew exactly how much money we had to play with in our journey to find our perfect house.

I was surprised at how upset I became when I learned that this happened to Kelly. I wanted to go over to this real estate office and give them a piece of my mind, but

Kelly also made me see the light: spend your energy where it is most impactful. We moved on. So, the next story, the next adventure, was not so surprising.

Journal: How often does this happen? How do you think we got these "all blank" neighborhoods?

DO YOU HAVE ANY IDEA THE STARTING PRICES OF THE HOUSES IN THIS DEVELOPMENT?

Despite her recent challenging real estate agent encounter, Kelly stepped up the research. With maps and newspapers including highlights and red circles strewn about our small living room, Kelly identified some interesting neighborhoods and cross-checked them with open house announcements.

The first neighborhood she found was close to the airport and relatively new. We pulled up and parked right in front of the model. As we got out and looked around, we both agreed it seemed nice: wide streets, sidewalks, mature trees. The houses looked different from each other, not cookie cutter. We walked up to the model home and walked in. We were immediately greeted by a younger, pretty hostess-like-person with a face of indifference. You expect a hostess to be happy, smiling, bubbly, with a friendly warm attitude.

"Excuse me, but do you know what the starting prices are of the homes in this development?"

Kelly looked at me with a face of *what is happening right now?* A half smile of confusion appears on her face.

"Do we know the starting prices of the homes in this development? Ouch, really?" I repeated. Always repeat what you heard so we are all on the same page. I am amped up. Kelly knows to get out of the way.

"We saw your advertisement in the newspaper, and it included the prices. Not to mention, we came with knowledge of what we are prequalified for." (Not that I would give you one penny right now.) I think, *Would I show a house to my new bride and then after she falls in love with the house say, yeah, but we can't afford it.*

"You can't ask that question," I added with agitated emphasis. "Wow. Do you understand that what you just asked us is illegal? You can't look at us as we pull in and park and decide by our looks, appearance, maybe our age, the car we drive what we can and cannot afford! I call this a visual credit check. Anyone who comes to visit your nice neighborhood has a legal right to take a look at what you are offering here, and you cannot stop us, dissuade us, or imply that we are in the wrong place. You are violating the Fair Housing Standards Act, and now I want to talk to your boss, whoever is running the place." There are things you *never* say or ask. Of course, the prospective buyers *prefer* to be treated with respect and dignity.

She was startled. "Wait a minute."

"You have a couple minutes before I call the feds and shut this place down!" I was lying of course, but I wanted her to think that we were ghost shoppers or auditors with the federal government, raising my voice for all around to hear.

She departed, and her boss came out hastily. "I think there has been a misunderstanding here."

"You think?" I replied with a stern look on my face.

The boss was very apologetic, stuttering, "Ah, I am so sorry. I will talk to our greeter." Then suddenly this manager guided us on a personally led tour in a golf cart, offered sandwiches, we got balloons, and he even offered us T-shirts (like I want a T-shirt, maybe to use it to check my dipstick). I told him his greeter was going to get him closed down.

Afterward, back in the car, Kelly asked, "What was that?"

I told her I put the fear of God in them; they believed we could inform the "Fair Housing Standards People" of the shit show they were running there.

Kelly went on to comment, "After a little prodding, they rolled out the red carpet, huh?"

"Yes, they knew that we knew what they were doing was wrong, illegal, disrespectful, and to me just infuriating."

I told Kelly we would never go back there and we would tell everyone we knew to stay away from that neighborhood. Again, another dynamic that contributes to how we get all blank neighborhoods. Salespeople with toxic attitudes and behaviors telling people where they can and cannot live is a horrible example of toxic discretionary power. Just disgusting, if you ask me.

When I look back at this sad adventure, I am struck by how quickly I felt so angry. Many people are told, "Don't get angry, don't be uppity, don't let them see you sweat, don't prove to them you are not worthy to be here." I had to "leave a mark." I had to nuke the place and leave no doubt in their minds that what they were doing was just wrong and illegal. I felt great about how I left the situation: speaking my mind, telling truth to discriminatory power. No regrets looking back.

From the United States Department of Justice's Civil Rights Division, The Fair Housing Act, 42 U.S.C. 3601 et seq., "prohibits discrimination by direct providers of

housing, such as landlords and real estate companies as well as other entities, such as municipalities, banks or other lending institutions and homeowners' insurance companies whose discriminatory practices make housing unavailable to persons because of:
- race or color
- religion
- sex
- national origin
- familial status, or
- disability."[2]

Journal: How often do you think this happens? Do you see exclusive neighborhoods, enclaves, and do you think the discriminatory dynamics I talk about are happening in that neighborhood? How many stand up to these forces whereas how many people just leave, saying nothing?

My parents "made it." They bought a house in a great neighborhood (McLean, Virginia). It was an idyllic safe hood, right? This is one of the most expensive zip codes in all of the state of Virginia. But even here, a Latino family, an immigrant family, had our toxic moments of "not feeling welcome."

GO BACK TO YOUR COUNTRY!

I was eight years old. We were walking home from something. Papa was holding my little hand when a pickup truck full of young men (older kids in my eyes) in the back of the truck pulled up and stopped. They were yelling at Papa. Out of nowhere we had this abrupt altercation.

"Go back to your country! You are not welcome here!"

I looked up at Papa, and I was asking him, "What are they saying and why are they saying this to us?"

He looked at me briefly, then turned to the pickup truck. Now you have to understand, this is McLean, Virginia, a nice neighborhood, and these kinds of run-ins were very rare. We were one of the only non-White, Hispanic families in the neighborhood. I guess we stuck out like a sore thumb.

Papa said, with a concern in his voice I rarely hear, "Listen, I am a vet, air force, Korea, this is my country. I served. Did you serve?"

The agitator in the back of the pickup truck looked at Papa with a puzzled look on his face and replied "Oh, you are a vet? Oh, okay, you can stay."

Papa asked again, "Are you a veteran?"

"Ah, no." He banged the cab of the pickup truck, and they drove off.

I asked again, "What were they saying, and why were they saying it to us?"

Papa said, "Tell you later; let's get home." We never spoke of this incident again.

I would realize later in life that there is bigotry all around us and that the wild card of dealing with these haters is to remind people of the fact that my father was a veteran. You see, my father and mother had come to our great country (legally) and my father had learned English quickly and then joined the air force and served at the tail end of the Korean War. He would then go to college on the GI Bill and graduate from Queens College, Queens, New York, at age thirty-two.

Journal: My father was masterful at dealing with conflict head-on. Maybe that is why I turned out to be a diversity and inclusion trainer and consultant; my father role modeled appropriate behaviors from when I was very little. Do you have someone like that in your life?

So we are not supposed to be in our nice neighborhood; even in school there are toxic people who want to make you feel unwelcome and inferior.

This whole book is about skilling you up. Empowering you with a set of skills and tools to employ in any and all situations where toxic behaviors are coming at you. Practicing and mastering these skills gives you confidence, courage to engage, to confront the toxic people in your life. My father was masterful, often staying calm but responding, not reacting. He had a temper but tried to keep it in check.

Journal: Do you walk away, or do you stand up to these institutional forces excluding and discriminating against people?

This chapter was about nonwork, real-life moments of toxicity. These moments can really influence one's life's journey. The next chapter presents some of the worst, most toxic people and toxic behaviors that I have ever encountered in my professional life.

CHAPTER 10.

COACH HIM BUT WE CAN'T FIRE HIM

When you go into a consulting and coaching situation, and the client limits some of your options right up front, you know it is not going to be smooth sailing. These stories are some of the most complicated situations I have ever had to face. Before I start, the client tells me, "We want you to meet this senior person, coach them, but we can't fire them; they are too important to this organization." It was like tying my hands behind my back. I share these stories to show you how I maneuvered through these various minefields.

NOW YOU CAN'T FIRE HIM BUT...

So, I have this client, a medical group. The CEO calls me, and the first thing he says to me is, "I have this one doctor who needs your help, but we can't fire him. He is highly specialized (only a few doctors with his unique technical skill set in the whole country), and it took us years to get him to come join our group. But he needs, we need, your help."

The doctor in question had a huge ego, thought he was smarter than everyone else and the things he said and did (because he knew he would not be fired) were horrific. Mostly sexist comments. A cocky, self-involved egotistical doctor who thinks they have great bedside manner, but really don't, is a recipe for disaster.

What finally got the client to act was that on one particular day, he decided to start his patient meetings with this phrase: "Spread your legs open like your mother never told you to."

Yes, the parent and the nurse were present in each encounter. Eight straight patients on one particular day endured this verbal harassment, this abuse, this just horrible display of toxic sexism.

Of course, the parents of the patients lost their minds. Complaints were filed. The nurse present could confirm what happened in each incident. I was asked to "curb his behavior, shape his behavior. Get him to stop!"

So we met and of course this doctor played dumb, aloof. "What is this all about?" he asked. "Why are we meeting?"

Really? Come on now, I thought. I told him that his actions had consequences, consequences he would feel and his employer was having to deal with, and that I was asked to remedy the situation. He looked at me with this cocky half smile, like he knew one of the remedies could not include him being fired. You know that "you can't fire me" look.

I told him I had run this by his CEO and human resources already. "For every complaint made about you, for every horrible thing you say or do, you will be fined and the monies will come out of your next paycheck. Your actions will have consequences (regardless of your intent, God help us trying to understand his intent). We are going to start at $500 for your first offense. Every complaint thereafter, the penalty, the consequence will go up in $500 increments." Like a toxic auction.

This doctor looked at me with this "yeah, sure," expression on his face. He listened quietly and the call was over. I had to point out to him that these issues could become public, and with social media it would become a huge embarrassment to the employer and his brand and reputation. He did not seem fazed. Weeks passed. Then I got the call.

"Mauricio, the wife of Doctor So-and-So on line one."

Hmm, I wondered, *this is going to be interesting.*

"Yes, this is Mauricio Velásquez, President of DTG. How can I help?"

The wife of Doctor So-and-So went on to tell me that "her husband's paycheck was $10,000 light. We can't make our mortgage, car (he drove a fancy car of course) or beach house payments."

I replied, "What did human resources say to you? Did you call them first?"

"Yes, I did, and they told me to call you for an explanation."

"Wow, okay. Let's start from the beginning. I was brought in to consult and coach on an emerging series of issues with your husband and his bedside manner. I am sorry to tell you, but your husband can be a narcissistic sexist, a real nightmare whose comments and behaviors can come across as really disgusting, offensive, and upsetting to patients and staff. I was instructed by his employer that we could not fire him because of his very special skill set and background, but something had to be done." I told her everything.

She replied, "I had no idea, but now that I know, I got this." I could hear her voice, the volume of her voice, energy just pop over the phone. She shared some rather saucy words with me that she would share with her husband "later today" and hung up.

Of course, at the end of the day Doctor So-and-So called, furious with me. He was yelling over the phone.

"Now hold on a second," I said in a calm voice. "All of this is happening because of your actions. Are you upset that your actions have consequences?"

"Well, I kind of get that, but my wife is furious with me. I am headed home now to a buzz saw of accountability and abuse."

I replied, "It is all about consequences. Now this is your problem and not my concern, all based on your actions. Good luck!"

You see, sometimes it takes a village to wrestle to the ground these toxic perpetrators and their behaviors. Happy to report, last I heard "he has been behaving himself." Every Toxic Superman has their kryptonite. So often in my work, it is the highly educated, highly skilled, and experienced toxic person and their behaviors that is the hardest nut to crack.

I did not think I would enlist his wife in the solution to this problem. It did not cross my mind, but once she called me, I was like "let's go all the way here and go for the jugular." This doctor was pretty hot with me—very angry at me for a long time, I was told. He made a bed he did not want to sleep in. The client was ecstatic with the results.

Here are the techniques I have presented in this book in their full glory. First is the I-Message, then the Stop-Start, and I finish with the Prefers and Nevers technique.

You are a highly competent, experienced doctor. (Start with a positive)

When you say sexist things to your patients, especially to minors with parents and a nurse present, you create a very difficult and potentially litigious situation complete with ample witnesses to hold you and this organization to account. We would prefer you stay away from said sexist comments and conduct.

We share this with you to be more self-aware and improve your bedside manner with more respectful banter. (End with positive)

More direct…

Please stop saying anything that could be construed as sexist, misogynistic, or even just rude or disrespectful.

Please start being more respectful, more professional and continue to give your practice your best effort and show your commitment to respect and dignity in the patient room.

We *prefer* you to be respectful, decent, cordial and keep the relationship focused on care.

We *never* want to hear that your conduct is sexist, misogynistic, or disrespectful.

The next story is the angriest person I have ever coached.

Journal: Know a person or situation like this, and if leadership had known sooner, maybe they would have "seen the light sooner"?

THIS IS ALL YOUR FAULT!

I often coach senior leaders. Lower-level people usually just get fired for their toxic antics. All too often, I meet with a senior person, someone their employer "wants to save, invest in them a little to correct or change their behaviors." Odd thing here: I am supposed to coach the person, tell the person I am presenting items for discussion and coaching that everyone else up to this point has been afraid to bring up with this person. The client, human resources, often tells me everything, and then I have to communicate to the target, the object of the coaching work. I guess I am the outside or third party "truth teller"; I truly have to speak truth to power. But here is the kicker: I don't change people; they have to change themselves. I create a coaching environment (actions and consequences) where I hope they chose to change their behavior pattern.

In this coaching scenario, I was meeting with a difficult CEO. He came into my office very reserved, gruff, quiet; he was keeping his cards close to his vest. He did not look happy to be meeting with me (although very few I have ever coached are). In my coaching sessions, I typically share a great deal about myself first before I ask the person to tell me about themselves, their background, their family, their career trajectory, etc.

I try to be authentic, genuine, vulnerable, really share things like: I am a sleepwalker; I was a geek/nerd/runt growing up; my parents are immigrants and how they raised me to respect people, treat all with dignity, you are not better than anyone else, just work hard and let your work speak for yourself, etc. I always make this the cornerstone of my introduction to build rapport.

We get into his background, his family, his work trajectory—and he blows up. Not sure what was the trigger. He came loaded for bear. A lot of pent-up anger just emerged abruptly.

The anger is now coming to the surface. This CEO yells at me, "There is no truth anymore. It is all about perspective. I am here because of you and your field. You diversity and inclusion trainers are opportunists, have turned these issues into a cottage industry. This is your fault that we have to meet and go through these hoops. I did not mean to offend her or anyone."

He had told someone on his staff who is gay that "he did not believe in her lifestyle and it was not right, they were an abomination, not Christian, and in the bible..."

"What? My fault? These issues you are talking about have been around a lot longer than my field. I mean hate, anti-LGBTQIA+ bias, resentment, political and religious strife, all opportunities for violence, existed long before I was even born. Justifying your hate issues through your own religious lens is why so many are abandoning traditional religions in our society. Hiding your hate inside your religion has been around since the beginning of time, wars, conflict. My fault, come on. Your actions have consequences. I was not there."

This CEO was fuming. "What I mean is, I said something, did something, and the person who complained twisted it."

I followed up with, "You have a right to say and do whatever you want, but you cannot control how your comments, your actions, are received."

"She took it the wrong way. Not what I meant—"

I interrupted him.

"She has no idea what you meant. At minimum, your comments, your actions, were insensitive, inappropriate, and definitely not work-related. What are you doing talking about, asking about, such personal questions as one's sexual orientation and then sharing your judgment, your opinion, of said orientation based on your faith and your religion?"

"My faith is very important to me," this CEO told me.

"Sure it is, but is sharing your faith, projecting your judgment, justifying your opinion with your faith appropriate at work? In essence, is imposing your faith, your religion, on other people you work with appropriate? Do you think this conversation is work-related, or even civil? Let me say this another way. You are a Christian, to be a Christian is to be Christlike. Do you think Jesus Christ would have said what you said, and how you said it to this person in the workplace, to your colleague? Would he have shared his opinion, his judgment, told this person their lifestyle is a sin, an abomination at work?" Although it was a rhetorical question, he seemed to understand.

"I thought we were close, I thought we had a good relationship and I could tell her, say almost anything."

"You are the CEO, you are not the everyday general rank and file employee here. You are the leader of this whole firm."

He was getting angry, and I was just bringing up the facts. "Because of your field, we can't have these kinds of profound conversations anymore. This wokeness is just killing me. You are twisting my words. That is not what I said or did."

All I did was repeat what he said. By the way, often the person I am coaching denies the fact pattern. Yet, when someone I am coaching says, "I did not mean to offend anyone," I say, "Okay, then, you admit you said it, you admit to what you did."

"She is taking this out of context, she is changing the meaning of what I said. There is no truth anymore."

"Oh, so you are saying wokeness is this notion of being too sensitive, overly sensitive? You cannot tell other people how to feel." The first coaching session was hostile in nature. He stood at times, yelling and pointing fingers at me.

"This is your fault we have to go through this coaching process." He kept bringing up politics. I told him politics, conversations about politics, can polarize, separate, and pit parties against each other. Politics are divisive right now, and I am always trying to unify parties and not allow them to stay separate and be opposed to each other.

The second coaching session was the tipping point, the point of transformation. He told me, "I have had time to reflect on what we discussed," as we started our second meeting in my office.

He started with a heartfelt apology, at least I felt he was sincere. I learned besides my feedback, human resources and other senior leaders had spoken to him privately. Getting constructive feedback from many different sources including a third-party source like me can really make a difference. Making sure the toxic person understands that no one in their organization is okay with what he said, it is not work-related, it violates their core values, and his actions are very inconsistent with their mission. Not to mention there was the possibility of further employment action.

It turns out he was demoted, and I suspect he felt fortunate it was a teachable moment. There was a history, a pattern, of related behaviors. He was being given another chance. He was calmer, smiling a little bit in our second session together. He acknowledged that many of my points made sense after thinking about them over a couple of days. I accepted his apology. He was an intellectual and needed time to process, he said.

We closed with him admitting to all of his comments, to the consequences of those comments, and I made him admit my field had nothing to do with his actions but this coaching could be a part of the remedy. We split on good terms. All the people I coach—we keep in touch. I tell all the people I coach, "Call me any time, for any reason, no charge," and some have.

Your personal values can be at odds with your corporate values but the corporate values in the workplace are what matters, what have weight and are more relevant and important than your personal values unless they are aligned.

Journal: Have you come across this interchange between religion, faith, and respect that is at the center of so much conflict and strife in our society? How did you deal with it?

Again, here are the techniques I have presented in this book in their full glory. We start with the I-Message, then follow with the Stop-Start and end with the Nevers and Prefers technique.

You are very valued Senior Member of Leadership. (Start with positive)

When you bring up your personal religious beliefs in the workplace and try to explain how you judged and condemned this person based on religious beliefs, I feel your comments are not respectful, are destructive, and could be seen as illegal in the workplace.

We would prefer you keep these comments to yourself and outside the workplace and focus your efforts on work-related matters.

We tell you this because we truly believe you have a great deal to offer as a mentor and technical leader in the organization. (End with a positive)

More direct...

Please stop sharing your personal faith, religion, and judgment with others in this workplace.

Please start focusing on the work, our mission, and the more technical aspects of our work where you are considered a real expert.

Continue to give this organization your full commitment and effort.

We *never* want to hear that you are discussing and imposing your faith, your religion, on other people.

We *prefer* you keep the conversations with our team members cordial, respectful, and professional.

HE LIKES TO WARN PEOPLE RIGHT UP FRONT

There are toxic people who believe if they warn you before they say or do something terrible, something inappropriate, that the parties warned cannot get offended. Not just once, but there is always a pattern of behavior: many events are linked together. This has crossed my desk many times, so many different coaching opportunities, way too many to count throughout my career. Especially as it relates to the gender specific harassment work I do: Harassment Prevention Training, Executive Coaching, and Expert Witness Testimony.

"I have a hilarious raunchy story to tell, so if you have thin skin you might want to leave the room!" Then this party just launches into the story. A seasoned veteran of this organization, he thinks his tenure provides him some latitude.

I typically start my assessment or investigation with, "So let me get this straight. You said this? And to whom? How many times? Every time, you warned your colleagues in the room before you started this sexist, racist, disgusting joke or story, right?" Corroborate, confirm facts. They usually own it because there are many parties, many witnesses, who can corroborate the events.

"Yes, I did not just want to drop the bomb, surprise people, I wanted to warn people so they would not get offended. You know, they could put up their shields, thicken their skin. I start all of our meetings with a joke or story. I like to start a meeting with a laugh."

This is a pattern of behavior, a pathology, a string of stories over a longer period of time. We connect the dots in my field, what the attorneys will do in the courtroom. Sometimes it is just one comment, "a slip on a banana peel," and the accountability is a "slap on the hand." Now with a pattern of behavior, we are in a different ball game.

"Warning people up front does not diminish the toxic impact of your comments. You also cannot tell other people how to feel. You start all or most of your meetings with a disgusting, not work-related story? Does not matter if you get a laugh!" Some would argue they laughed under duress, or it was a nervous laugh. He is their boss.

"Yes, almost every meeting. I think I can tell a good story. Well, no, not everyone laughs." He pauses, almost like a stutter.

"You have been doing this for how long? No one has ever told you this was inappropriate at best, illegal at worst? Did you read the room, look at the body language of everyone present? Or are you emotionally illiterate, unaware of how your comments, stories, made people feel?"

"I like a certain level of sexual tension in the workplace. I am a joker, a kidder, a clown, everyone knows that about me." That is the problem, and the employer had never rolled out harassment prevention training.

"What? Are you kidding me? Are you listening to what you just said? Do you understand the pertinent laws here?" I walked him through Title VII of the 1964 Civil Rights Act.

"I had no idea I was offending people, hurting people, making people feel uncomfortable. I did not know my actions were so toxic. I mean, you need to have some thick skin when you work with me. Nobody said anything."

"Unbelievable. And you think you are not responsible or liable here? You are going to get fired and the targets, the plaintiffs, can go after your personal assets."

"I had no idea."

"Now that is your problem; ignorance is not bliss, won't get you out of legal trouble. It's like telling the officer after being pulled over, 'I was driving so fast, I did not see the speed limit sign, I could not read it.' No!" He did not want to apologize for his actions, he had this "I am what I am attitude," and he actually said, "They would not fire me; I am a top performer." Such an ego.

With that, our meeting was over, and I recommended he be demoted; again, I was told he would not be let go.

One last time in this chapter are the techniques I have presented in this book in their full glory. Same order: I-message first, then Stop-Start, and we finish with the Prefers and Nevers.

You are revered for your technical expertise. (Start with a positive)

When you warn people right up front that you might offend them with this pending story or joke, I feel you think that protects you from accountability.

I would prefer you understand that you are actually explaining your intent up front and worsening the impact of your actions. You are actually making this worse and amplifying the consequences of your stories.

You are getting corrective feedback because we believe you can learn and grow from this experience.

More direct...

Stop with any sexist or racist or any other inappropriate, not respectful banter, small talk, or storytelling.

Start focusing on our clients, our work, and our mission.

Continue to add value, to use your technical background to advise and consult with our team members.

We *prefer* you be respectful and decent and stay professional at all times.

We *never* want to hear that you are still telling your stories or jokes and warning people ahead of time. Refrain completely from such inappropriate and unprofessional conduct.

Journal: Have you ever met someone so tone deaf, so out of touch? A person who is not reading the room.

Now we turn from some of the most challenging moments of my career to the most unexpected, most surprising outcomes of my career.

CHAPTER 11.

THINK LIKE A WORKPLACE INVESTIGATOR

Among the many hats I wear is one as a workplace investigator. Organizations often want an objective third party outside the organization who can come in and add value. They want me to come in and conduct an informal and quick "360 degree evaluation" and then start coaching this person.

It has always helped me and it can help you to think like a workplace investigator. I want to share some lessons learned from my investigation and coaching processes.

The first and most fundamental question you must ponder throughout your situation, the investigation process, is this: If you are the victim, the target of bullying and toxic behaviors, is it safe to say something, to stand up for yourself? Are you working in a psychologically safe workplace? This is a critical concept in understanding the culture, the workplace environment where toxic behaviors and moments of truth are allowed to fester and take root.

I really appreciate the work of Amy Edmondson, the Harvard Business School professor and author of

The Fearless Organization, who coined the phrase "team psychological safety." Dr. Edmondson says, "Team psychological safety is a shared belief held by members of a team that it's okay to take risks, to express their ideas and concerns, to speak up with questions, and to admit mistakes—all without fear of negative consequences." As Edmondson puts it, "it's felt permission for candor."[1]

Could the people being targeted, victimized by the toxic person, say something? Push back? Or was it not safe?

Often people will say to me in the interview process, "He is a jerk or a bully but that is not illegal, is it?" It is not illegal to be a jerk in general, but it is illegal to be a jerk to a protected class. Everyone has a right to a respectful, toxic-free workplace. Whenever you are being mistreated, demeaned, degraded, belittled, pull out a pad or a cell phone, and start taking notes. When the toxic person sees you taking notes it might make them pause, reflect, or even stop their behavior entirely. Ask yourself these investigatory questions.

WHAT JUST HAPPENED TO ME?

Focus on actions and behaviors (not guessing or surmising intent behind actions).

Note the date, time, place.

Has this toxic behavior happened before? Is there a pattern, a pathology of behavior?

Who else is present (witnesses to corroborate or confirm what just happened)?

How did other people react to the toxic conduct?

Do we have an anti-bullying policy? A relatively new development in human resource policies and procedure world.

Collect evidence. Collect emails, texts, voice mails, notes, cards, any proof that is contributing to you feeling uncomfortable or, as my daughter says, "creeping me out."

Take notes, document everything as soon as things develop, and try not to rely on your memory days or weeks later.

I have seen people turn on their phone: be careful of legality (I am not an attorney), but a recording can prove what happened. It may not be admissible in court (varies by state), but human resources will want to hear your recording.

In so many situations where I am conducting an investigation, often the toxic person would say, "Never happened, I did not say or do that. This person is making this whole thing up." Toxic people, they can be just straight up liars. With a recording from your phone, we have them in the lie. We can fire them for lying. This has happened many times in my career.

Look, investigations have three outcomes. We can prove what was alleged occurred, we can prove what was alleged is a lie, a fabrication (false accusation), or we can't prove either way. Often, perpetrators will try and cover up their toxic acts, and it is the cover-up that gets them in more trouble.

Let me start with two of my most powerful coaching experiences. In these stories, there was some denial but also some ample evidence, serious allegations and real serious evidence available.

MY DEPUTY NEEDS COACHING!

The executive director (ED) of a major not-for-profit reached out to me.

"My deputy, our number two, needs some help. What do you typically do, what is your approach?"

"Well, I interview you, his boss, several peers, and three to five of his direct reports, his subordinates, one-on-one. It is a very informal 360 assessment. I pick the questions and send them to the target of the coaching to review. I meet with each person in an out-of-the-way conference room, keep them anonymous, and as they are answering the questions, I am typing their answers into my laptop. My laptop is connected to a big screen or projector, and as the interviewees are talking their answers are appearing up on the screen. They can see it is anonymous; no name will appear anywhere in the document. This transparency promotes trust and understanding."

I say to the ED, "I figure this will take a day to gather the data, and then I will share it with both you and the coaching target."

The executive director says with urgency, "Good, fine, make it happen."

I send the questions ahead to the executive director, and he shared them with his deputy, the target of the coaching effort. When we meet the person I am to coach, he says to me, "I like your questions. I want to add a couple, and I have identified thirty-two people for you to interview."

"Thirty two interviewees?" I respond. "Well, I have to go back to your boss and get authorization for thirty-two participants. I was going to interview eight initially."

I go back to his boss, the executive director, and he says, "Sure, fine, whatever he wants, just do it." I point out this is not a day of work but now a week. He nods as I leave his office. I am there all week.

First, to make sure the interviews generate honest and authentic responses to the questions, I ensure the interviews are anonymous. I tell people as they walk in: "Please don't tell me your name." As they settle in, they see my laptop is plugged into a projector and their answers will appear on the screen (again, their name is not up there). I even had one client put a wall in the room; I sat on one side of the wall, the interviewee sat on the other side of the wall, and we both could see the screen but not each other (like the Dating Game). I also point out "it is really not about what one person says, but more about what issues keep coming up over and over again." Please note these are all open-ended questions intended to draw in the broadest array of answers (no leading questions here).

1. What are this person's strengths?
2. What is this person doing well?
3. What does this person need to know about his/her management approach and leadership style?
4. Where could she/he improve in general?
5. Where can she/he improve specifically, behaviorally?
    - What she/he should *stop* doing to improve our relationship and team dynamics?
    - What she/he should *start* doing (in lieu of what they stop) to improve our relationship and team dynamics?
    - What she/he should *continue* doing that presently is a good foundation for building upon?
6. Do you trust this person? Yes or no and why? Looking for a set of behaviors here. What do they do that builds trust? What do they do that undermines trust?

7. If we broke down all the behaviors that this person exhibits in the workplace, what behaviors do you *prefer* to see, to experience, to be exposed to everyday and what behaviors do you *never* want to see, experience, or be exposed to again?
8. In your opinion, what is one change that this person could make to his/her approach, his/her management style that would have the greatest impact on how she/he adds value here at x organization?
9. Anything else you would like to tell me? Please take advantage of this process, this opportunity.

On Friday, at the end of a long week of interviews, I tell the deputy, "Listen, give me the weekend to summarize these interviews, and on Monday you will get my report and we'll go from there."

The deputy says, "Oh no, I would like to see the raw data." This happens from time to time when the target of the coaching process wants to see the raw data and not just the summary report. The executive director was getting a copy of each interview via email after each interview. I asked the executive director's permission, and he allowed his deputy to see the raw data. The deputy reviewed all the interview data over the weekend.

The data was awful. This deputy is a bully, manipulative, has no interpersonal skills, is really hard to "read" and to work with, and all thirty-two interviews are just brutal and unforgiving. Toxic with a capital T.

On Monday, I am called into the executive director's office and the first thing he says before I can even sit down is, "Deputy resigned last night."

"No way, what?" I am thinking here is where I am going to get fired. He surprises me.

"Mauricio, great work!"

"Sorry, what?"

"Mauricio, this is exactly what I wanted to happen. He needed to go, and I did not have the heart to tell him. We have known each other for many, many years and, quite frankly, I was not interested in paying him a large severance package."

"Wait, this was your end game the whole time? I would have appreciated a heads up."

"No, I know you and your process. I wanted it to be pure. You have a big heart, you are genuine, authentic, and sincere, and I knew if I tainted the process, biased you, this would not work. Mauricio, great work, you saved us a bundle. Your fees are nothing compared to the severance we would have had to pay him. I will be in touch."

I walked out with this look on my face. *What just happened?* The strangest backhanded compliment I have ever received in my career. To this day, I tell my clients "to trust the process," and I share this story as proof.

This is one of the highlights of my career. I always say, "Let's follow the data, see where the feedback takes us." The power of coaching, the impact of feedback, especially from a third party, an objective "outsider," can be very insightful, very enlightening (if the coaching target internalizes the findings). There is no denying it; this can be a very powerful, life-changing event.

Journal: Do you have someone in your organization who really needs coaching or just needs to leave (quit or be fired), but no one will tell him/her?

ANYBODY BUT MAURICIO

I was brought in by a client to conduct an investigation. It was presented as a 360 coaching process, but it was more of an investigation. The entire team had threatened to resign all at once if something was not done immediately. The party in question was revered for her understanding of the work, her work experience, her background; technically, she was above reproach.

She had a temper. She could be intense. Early on, her team thought "she was committed to the work, our mission." But quickly perceptions changed, feelings were hurt, and hurt turned to anger and frustration (typically does), and an "all hands mutiny" developed. Oddly enough, she had united her team against her (weird way to build a team). They were so organized that they had all talked and approached the director of this area and threatened to quit en masse if things did not change. A letter with specifics, a petition so to speak, was sent to the director. Now, the director could not just fire her: she was too valuable to the agency, I was told.

She was the smartest, technically most talented person in the room. However, she was known for cursing, flipping the bird, throwing furniture. She would even come into the men's room looking for a member of her team. She was a gossip, spoke about her own team behind their backs to other members of the team, and they would share what she said. Toxicity at the highest level.

Few people can take this much abuse without just saying to themselves, "What am I doing here?" But we are talking about professionals; the work was piling up and needed to get done. If they all quit together, there would be huge ramifications for this agency. I interviewed all parties involved, and I recommended she be removed from her managerial, leadership role. I put this in writing per their request. Some clients want nothing in writing, not this client.

"I think cattle are treated better," I quipped on a call. Since termination was not an option, I did not recommend it. I recommended she be put in a technical role with no direct reports and that she received intense and regular executive coaching, especially if down the line they were going to put her back in a managerial role.

When they asked her who she would like her coach to be she said, "Anybody but Mauricio."

I was hired soon thereafter. Challenging, difficult at first, tense does not begin to describe those early coaching sessions, but we persevered. Her pushback was always: "I had no idea" and "I meant no harm."

"No one can read your mind," I reiterated. "Your intentions are not relevant."

I quickly moved her focus to her actions and the consequences of her actions. We discussed at great length the Prefers, behaviors people who work with her prefer to see, and the Nevers, behaviors she can never exhibit again (risk of being terminated if these behaviors continue). We got through it together. We went from a no-trust, high-suspicion relationship to one of profound trust and understanding. We stay in touch through Facebook, and I know she has gone on to have a successful career.

Deep down, she was in pain, and people in pain hurt others; she was hurting and in turn hurt others. There was a lot going on at home. Unfortunately, she was bringing these issues, transferring, projecting these toxic feelings and behaviors to the workplace. And that is never acceptable, especially in the long run.

A FAITH-BASED RACIST

I was hired to investigate a particular prickly supervisor. As is always my approach, I interviewed everyone who worked in that particular department. A new hire was coming on board, and the supervisor was very excited about this new hire until he did some personal research. He went onto social media to "check this new hire out."

It turns out this new hire is White and is married to an African American woman. The supervisor just blew up, telling everyone who worked there that the new hire coming on board shortly was in a mixed-race marriage and the supervisor did not approve. In the interview, he did not deny his actions. Everyone on the team confirmed what he had done and said, and they are all quite puzzled at his actions. Mixed-race relationships and marriages are not uncommon in this town. Also, everyone tells the new hire what the new supervisor is saying about him behind his back.

This supervisor tells me he is a "God-fearing man," and his faith does not allow him to be around, work with, or support mixed-race families. I was perplexed. This is blatant racism, and he did not deny it.

I was fired up by this point in the interview, and I told the supervisor, "I have never come across a situation like this where the hiring authority digs up dirt on the new hire prior to them arriving and spreads gossip and judgment about the new hire. This is blatant racism, and that is just plain illegal!"

Nothing burns me up more than people hiding their hate inside their religion, using their religion, their faith, to justify their hate. This is all too common in our country right now.

His response was, "Well, I don't see it that way."

I replied, "I don't care how you see it, this is how human resources, leadership, heck even the courts will see it. Not to mention what does his race or his relationship have to do with his job, his credentials, his qualifications and experience?"

He was terminated soon thereafter.

If they had kept him and I was his boss I would say...

You are clearly a valued member of this team, you are the supervisor.

When you spread racist remarks loaded with judgment about a new hire,

I feel you are instilling racism into the culture of this team and this is blatantly illegal.

I would prefer you look at each person on your team based on their capabilities, work effort, and results.

You are a decent supervisor and you should know racism has no place in this work environment.

More direct...

Please stop injecting racism into our team relationships and dynamics.

Please stop hiding your racism behind your faith.

Please start looking at each person based on their merits.

Never ever bring up racist comments again in this workplace.

Prefer you be more respectful and respect the dignity of all your team members.

In the next chapter, we ready ourselves for returning to our toxic work or home and being more skilled, more ready, to stand up for ourselves and against the toxicity in our lives.

CHAPTER 12.

GOING BACK INTO THE WORLD WITH YOUR EYES AND EARS WIDE OPEN

Story after story, I wanted you to be able to turn the toxic tide. With this book, I wanted people to take charge over their toxic relationships, be able to respond, not react, with skill, tactfully address the toxic person and their behaviors. I wanted you to be able to confront your bully, declaw your narcissist, stop the harassment, the hate, and the bigotry. Too many people suffer in silence, standing on the sidelines, and I wanted people to "get in the game" and go from bystander to upstander.

I hope you took notes so you could refer back to this book like a guide, a how-to resource. You have this book behind you now. You have read it front cover to back. Hopefully, you journaled certain critical thoughts and issues, solutions, and you can now take action. I hope you can relate to many if not almost all of the stories, my stories. My stories are your stories.

This book is about how to deal with each of these moments of toxic truth, and I wanted you to see how I dealt with them, what I said, what I did.

Now what is the opposite of being toxic? How about being present, making sure the people you work with and come across know you respect and value them, even total strangers. I try to make people feel seen, feel special. I am always heaping praise where I can. Giving positive feedback and reinforcing respectful behavior every day just feels good and should not be rare or odd.

You are doing an amazing job.

When you come in early, stay late, meet or exceed deadlines, I feel really proud to be on your team.

You are crushing it!

Have you opened the door for someone recently, helped a stranger and they were surprised? I was at a light and there was a guy trying to push his car into the gas station. He was stuck in the middle of the intersection. I pulled to the side, got out, and ran to him to help him push his car. I yelled at my kids in the car, "Let's go help this guy!" His face when all four of us came to his aid was priceless.

We are all on this planet together. Kindness, compassion, "paying it forward" should not be rare occasions; do it regularly, make someone else's day. Random acts of kindness should be more regular, more frequent, and less rare or random.

Be a professional; get the job done and do it in a positive way. Something bad is happening at home, leave it at home if you can. Or confide in someone, but your bad situation at home should not affect the people you work with in the office. Don't allow yourself to project your bad times at home and bring it to work; that is being an amateur and making excuses.

Some recent events come to mind.

MAKE THEIR DAY

I was at Washington Dulles Airport recently. Dulles was jam-packed on this particular afternoon, flights delayed everywhere, hot because the air conditioning was struggling to keep up with the heat and humidity outside, and just way too many people crammed in the terminals. Perfect conditions for potential toxicity and the tension were high.

Airports are a place where you can see and experience high levels of toxicity from complete strangers, and this story was fraught with wound up travelers on their last thread. I chose to take the high road of respect and dignity for all. I mean, I try to praise others, be positive, address people by their name, and make someone else's day. Yes, they are total strangers and why not.

Since my flight was so delayed, I decided to get some walking in, get my steps, and go to all three United Clubs in Terminals C and D and have a drink in each one—my own private pub crawl, so to speak. I had hours to burn. In the second club pub, I had this exchange.

"Abeba, thank you for the cold beer!" Abeba, my bartender, immediately lit up with a smile.

"Oh thank you, thank you for using my name!"

"Of course," I said.

In the airport men's room, I said to the janitor, "Paulo, this place is spotless, thank you."

He thanked me profusely for thanking him. No one is invisible, no one deserves to feel lesser than or inferior. Make their day, prop them up.

There was a traveler near the luggage carousel yelling at the porter as I was walking by. "Where is my luggage. Don't you know who I am?"

I find this absolutely absurd, comical really. I burst out laughing (loudly). He glanced at me, and he realized in that moment that I was laughing at him. A total stranger, fellow traveler, found his toxic antics hilarious. Humor is welcome at all times in the toxic times. Humor can defuse the tension.

Ouch, really. Yelling at a total stranger who has discretionary power over you in this situation? Amateur! I would send his luggage to the other side of the world if I was that porter. Always treat people with respect, especially people in high stress service jobs.

We are all human beings, and no one should be made to feel inferior, invalid, or not welcome. Tell that person you see them! I was raised to always address people by their name, especially among strangers or in service settings. Treat people with respect, always. Who do you think you are, anyway?

Be positive, be upbeat, smile and address people by their name, right? How hard is that? Are you too busy to show a little kindness? It is easy to be respectful, harder to be a jerk if you ask me. When I smile at others, I say something positive or uplifting and yes, I feel better inside.

I also thanked my travel compadres Gin and Tonic for their company on this recent travel adventure. Of course, on airplanes there is another level, a higher level of potential toxicity.

"GENTLEMEN, LET'S NOT GET KICKED OUT OF FIRST CLASS OR DELAY OUR DEPARTURE"

I am boarding a flight from Washington Dulles to Los Angeles. I'm on the Jetway, and two people in front of me are pushing each other (to get in front of each other in the line) and they almost get in a fight. How quickly these things go from zero to sixty. I think nothing of it. I'm just watching. I do love to people-watch, especially in an airport. So, I'm just observing, trying not to judge. I find our diversity, our different looks and appearances, so fascinating.

One of the two parties who nearly got in a fight, his name is on his leather jacket, so if he's trying to stay incognito or "not use his fame," he is terrible at it. He is a famous singer, a pop artist. Oh, and his eyes are so bloodshot red, he's definitely under the influence of something. I am that close to these two. He is slurring his words. By the way, he is not a tall guy; he's shorter like me. The other guy whom he was about to get into a tussle with was a solid six inches taller.

We board the 757. When you walk in, for first class you go left and for economy you go right. I go left (I had received an upgrade) with excitement; I always appreciate an upgrade to first class. The inebriated artist is in front of me and turns left into first class and he sits on the aisle (port side) in front of me and I sit down right behind him, on the next row on the aisle like him. Guess who comes up behind us?

The other guy, the big guy, whom he had almost tussled with is standing above him. *No, no* I say to myself, *you have to be kidding me. Of all the people to sit next to you is the guy you almost went to blows with just minutes earlier.* He walks right up to said star singer and says, "Hey, you are sitting in my seat!"

Now you can see that the prior scuffle is fresh in his mind. His face, his posture, he is just amped up. Said pop star looks up.

"No way man, I never sit in the window," the pop artist responds and begins to look for his boarding pass. Meanwhile, his fighting partner keeps repeating himself.

"You are in my seat, and you better move or there is going to be trouble!" He looks like he is puffing up like a puffer fish.

"No, no, man, I can't sit in the window seat." The pop artist continues to repeat himself, but his boarding pass does say (and I can see from my vantage point) that he is in the wrong seat. He stands face-to-face or rather face-to-chest with the other guy. I have to say something. I mean, I am right there watching this whole saga develop, and I cannot just watch them go to blows.

"Gentlemen, let's not get kicked out of first class or delay our departure over this, please. I mean, I don't think violence is going to get us anywhere but get kicked off the plane." Pop star looks at me.

"You know what, this guy is making sense to me. What is your name? (I tell him.) Mauricio (hacks my name with his slurred speech) here, my new friend, is right." And he moves over to the aisle seat. Now across the aisle from me is a relative or friend, part of his entourage (looked like his brother), who taps me on the shoulder and gives me a thumbs up.

If I told you said pop star was under the influence and did not move one muscle the rest of the flight, he passed out, would you be surprised? I mean, he might as well have been a piece of luggage. He missed all of the goodies in first class: more for the rest of us, I guess.

Travel is not what it used to be. I come across more people who are more wound up, tighter than ever these days. I always think, "Where are the professional travelers?" Also, sometimes you just have to lean in and say something or all of us will pay the price with a delayed departure.

Sometimes we have to support each other, people you don't even know. I always think of our common humanity; we all need a little support from a stranger sometimes.

A FEW WORDS ABOUT TRUST

I find toxic individuals whom I come across in my career to be people you don't trust. This lack of trust is corrosive to relationships and morale. The toxic people I have coached rarely consider whether their direct reports or colleagues trust them. If I don't trust you and you don't trust me, the rest of the relationship is doomed for failure.

Look at current events: no trust on Capitol Hill, no trust between Ukrainians and Russians, Israel and Palestine, and every day in the media we see people who don't trust the police or government. So much of the violence between total strangers can come down to "did they trust each other?" I just want to point this out because too many people I see don't see the connection between being toxic and a lack of trust.

Ask yourself: Do I trust this person? If not, what has the other person done, behaviorally, that leads you to feel this way. Actions have consequences. Look at your behaviors, look at how you treat people or how others treat you. SMR Covey's work and books on trust, *The Speed of Trust* and his newest book, *Trust and Inspire*, are fabulous reads.

Do the people I work with every day trust me? Ask them. Do you trust me? If not, how can I regain your trust? If you do trust me, what do I do every day that leads you to believe that I trust you? Ask yourself, *Do I trust them?* Convey to the people you work with every day what they do that makes you trust them.

You see with trust that toxicity disappears. We give each other the benefit of the doubt, we assume good intent behind any actions and behaviors, and suspicion or a lack of trust can never take hold.

Looking back at this book and looking at your life, you are now ready. Ready to conduct an inventory of the present state of your life.

YOUR WORK-LIFE INVENTORY

Is my workplace a safe place? Do I feel comfortable saying something to the toxic person?

In your workplace you must consider:

- First and foremost that it is safe to say something, to speak up in the moment of toxicity. At home or at church or wherever, do you have the multiple pathways, options to go seek help? You are not alone. Do you have someone you know whom you trust, whom you can go to and confide in and seek help and resolution? (Is human resources at work trusted? At church can you go to the pastor, or at home does someone in your family see what is happening and can they address it?)
- Is the workplace environment, the culture, respectful, fun, at ease? Yes, there are deadlines, stress, and pressure, but it should not drive anyone to be disrespectful, awful, or even hateful.
- Is there a clear, well-defined vision of what is respectful, a toxic-free workplace that looks like it is built on the core values of the organization?

- Do you have core values, do the organizations have a set of values including respect, dignity in the workplace (could say the same for the home front), and are they "lived values" and not just words on a piece of paper? Are people held to account if these values are violated, not lived?
- Do you have people you can go to outside the relationship you have with this toxic person? Is human resources open and amendable to listen to you and help you? Do you hear "hey, not our problem, you are on your own" or "We can help?"
- Does the organization have an ombudsman? Hot line? Ethics tip line? Toxic behaviors, left unaddressed, left to fester, can lead to harassment, discrimination, even violence in the workplace, and these systems are in place to make sure these things don't come to pass.
- Do you have a workplace bullying policy, a handbook that defines what is harassment?

At home, at church, at school, ask: Do I feel comfortable saying something? Typically, as a parent, you are stronger, more courageous when protecting your children. At church, can I go to our faith leader? Will he or she actually address the toxicity?

At home, do we deal with these issues head-on or do we look the other way? Do we sweep it under the rug and hope these toxic issues just go away by themselves (and we all know they rarely go away completely, by themselves: they often fester)?

EYES AND EARS WIDE SHUT:
THE SILENCE IS DEAFENING

I have always specialized in hostile or militant audiences, but from time to time even I have to step back and pause for a second. Current events are always fair game in my workshops; it's what makes my sessions electric and never boring. From the political tenor to the mass shootings to the horrible acts of hateful violence from Matthew Shepard to George Floyd and so many others, these current events come riddled with emotion and outrage for so many participants in my workshops.

Recent *moments of truth* in my sessions led me to pen and update the original article I wrote many years ago. The recent rash of horrible racial injustices (some say pattern) of Ahmaud Arbery to Breonna Taylor to George Floyd to Amy Cooper to Jacob Blake has erupted into a national conversation about racial injustice, white privilege, inequity, diversity, inclusion, civility, and more.

Comments like: "I don't care about Black Lives Matter, I am trying to run a business" or "White Lives Matter" or worse "White Lives Matter More" when people mention Black Lives Matter have led to the politicization and polarization of these horrible atrocities, and these acts continue a horrible pattern of racial injustice. You have to go back to "Rodney King had it coming!" and "Trayvon Martin, who cares." Today, you must be a "liberal" or a "conservative"—ouch!

I am so struck by the lack of empathy, the callousness, the insensitivity of these comments, but people are underestimating the passion, the energy, the rage behind all of this. Eyes and ears wide shut really. These horrible, just insensitive, racist, sexist, homophobic, ethnocentric comments are made almost daily, but where is the outrage, the condemnation, the "calling this person out?" All the "Anti-DEI" or "DEI Hire" rhetoric is just wrong and quite frankly disgusting. Let me be blunt here: too many of those opposing DEI efforts are really opposing what the DEI profession challenges in the workplace: favoritism, nepotism, harassment, discrimination, bullying, incivility, and the rest of it.

REMEMBER:
What you permit—you promote
What you allow—you encourage
What you condone—you own

The silence is deafening, quite frankly. Where are our leaders to unify and not polarize us? Where are the decent folk to call out these horrible comments and actions? Be that upstander and not a bystander. Be the change you want to see in others.

When these comments above were uttered in front of their peers, their colleagues (in a workshop), what struck me the most was the rest of the participants in the session did not even flinch when they heard these comments. Oh, and these comments are coming from people they know, people they work with every day, not some stranger. How do the individuals who don't agree with these remarks (or who are horribly offended, afflicted) interpret the silence of their peers? Tacit support. Agreement. Endorsement.

Toxicity is way up, and now is the time to use what you learned in this book to combat these toxic issues. How about an "ouch" or "wow" or "really" or "come on" or even a nonverbal reaction (facial expression, hand or body gesture)—some nonverbal action to show disapproval? Change the sound of your voice on a virtual call to convey your dislike and displeasure for the horrible comment. Oh, and stop with the "I did not say something because I thought I would get fired" comments. You are not going to get fired for saying "wow" or "ouch." Come on! Time to be a part of the solution and not contributing to the problem. Enablers, colluders, conflict avoiders are playing a big role in all of this. If you are not a part of the solution you are definitely a part of the problem.

We all need to step up and say something. Challenge the injustice, the lack of civility; speak up for those who don't have a voice. Haters (or what I prefer to call *toxic individuals*) win, get stronger, and are emboldened when they go unchallenged. It is a form of bullying or intimidation, and don't tell me I am making this up or blowing this out of proportion. Just look around, open your eyes and ears. Hate crimes are up, bullying, workplace violence, terrorism, hate groups, domestic terrorism, pick your poison—the symptoms, the manifestations, of hate and distrust are everywhere.

We all have a shared responsibility to lean in. I love these teachable moments that current events present us to stir the conversation. Don't pass up on the chance. I would rather my kids talk about these issues with me and we get it all out in the open than for them not to talk about it and freeze when someone else tries to blindside or ambush them.

It is when we all come to the aid of each other and not just step up to defend "one of our own" that unity and respect for all is practiced. When men stand up for women, White for Black, Brown for Black, Black for White, and the rest of the permutations (you know what I mean) and we all stand up for each other, then I will finally feel like we are getting somewhere. I have said this before—the greatest challenge to humanity is staying human.

We all have a shared responsibility to each other as human beings. I always find it odd when I am defending, challenging or coming to the aid of another and a person asks me, "Why do you care, you are not a (blank)?" We have to speak out for each other, especially for "those who are different" or for those who have less privilege or power.

Martin Niemöller's famous poem, "First They Came," is ringing in my ears as we finish here together. The poem mentions all the times the poet did not speak out and let others be oppressed and put in concentration camps and murdered during Nazi Germany. The final line, when he mentions that no one spoke up for him, shows how we are all connected.[1] Upstanding for others is upstanding for yourself. Too many of us have to stop being bystanders and become upstanders.

I hope I have helped you move from bystander to upstander. You are now skilled, equipped, to take the toxic behaviors you face head-on! It might be difficult at first, but stick to it, practice these techniques, use these tools I give you, and you will make a difference in this world. We need more fighters in this fight for dignity and respect for all.

WE ARE BUILDING A COMMUNITY!

I will be rolling out a regular podcast where people can check in, share their toxic situation, and we can work through it, address the situation, and resolve the conflict together in a safe, almost therapeutic forum-like atmosphere where we all learn and grow together.

I was thinking about rolling some annual awards: Most Toxic Situation and How You Dealt with This Person. No names, like a Dear Abby kind of podcast. Hope you join us! Visit Diversitydtg.com for more information. Want to reach out to me directly? mauriciov@diversitydtg.com.

INTERVIEWS

What the Interviews Revealed

INTERVIEWS—I interviewed industry professionals, human resource professionals, to get their perspectives.

You know, I just dove into this book and started writing, and the stories, the content was just pouring out of me; it was almost therapeutic or cathartic. Thanks to my publisher and my first editor. It was recommended that I conduct some interviews. I'd never ever thought of doing this before.

I was 30,000 words into this book before I started interviewing people. These are professionals from many industries who deal with toxic behaviors and toxic individuals on a regular basis. I had some premises, some hypotheses, some ideas (behind the writing of this book) that I wanted to test, to verify, to really explore and tackle.

I spoke to over two dozen professionals from over two dozen industries and, quite frankly, I stopped interviewing people because the answers were starting to converge on similar themes. I had found consensus, I had found confirmation and some nuanced insight.

For instance, I believe that toxic individuals and their behaviors in organizations, we typically know who these folks are but we don't deal with them, we ignore, we look away, because most people are conflict avoiders. Most people think, "If I just look away, pretend we don't have these issues of toxicity, they will just work themselves out and go away by themselves." Ridiculous, madness if you ask me.

I also believe many people don't know how to engage, don't know to address the toxic behaviors. We lack the skills and tools; we are not equipped to deal with the toxic set of behaviors or the toxic person exhibiting those behaviors. Part of this might be because the toxic person in question is a very powerful person: senior executive, matriarch or patriarch at home. No one wants to tell the emperor he has no clothes.

I think one of the most important questions I asked these professionals was the sixth question: "How do you prepare for a 'usual suspect,' someone you know is going to exhibit these toxic behaviors and be difficult in an upcoming meeting?" My findings are spread throughout the book, but I thought you would like to know, like to see the set of questions I asked and the themes and overall takeaways. I included my favorite quotes below and general themes of the answers to my questions. Can you relate to these comments?

INTERVIEW QUESTIONS:

1. **When you hear the phrase "toxic employee" or "toxic behaviors," what words pop into your head?**

"Poisonous. Shut off from emotions. They don't like themselves. Spread like wildfire. Want everyone around them to be unhappy (along with them) to make their toxicity comfortable."

Theme: Toxicity is highly contagious, and it often has something to do with their own insecurity (of the toxic person).

Training workshops we lead in Dealing with Toxic Individuals, Toxic Workplaces confirms the ease at which toxic people try to influence all of those around them, to bring them down, to suck the light out of the room.

2. **Do you believe most organizations know who their toxic employees/managers/leaders are, those exhibiting the morale-crushing toxic behaviors?**

"In my experience, organizations often have a sense of who may be exhibiting toxic behaviors, but the extent of awareness can vary. Identifying and addressing toxic behaviors require a combination of keen observation, open communication channels, and proactive leadership. Fear and denial are really powerful energies but prohibit us from dealing in reality. In general, we choose to look the other way."

Theme: Almost unanimously, every interviewee said they were aware of who their toxic employees, managers, and leaders are and often the telltale sign is high turnover in this toxic area of the organization.

Training workshops we lead in Dealing with Toxic Individuals, Toxic Workplaces are put on to help our clients' employees, supervisors, and mangers to deal with the workplace toxicity (rare client).

3. **Why does leadership in organizations and parents in families address or not address the toxic behaviors?**

"It is easier to turn a blind eye. We stand to lose. Fear and denial. We don't engage because we are too afraid.

In my family, I stood to lose by calling out my family members. They lack leadership skills. It all comes down to fear."

Theme: Fear and the consequences of holding people accountable protect the toxic person. Avoidance feels safer than engaging the toxic behaviors, so people look the other way. People lack courage, and I think it is due to their lack of skill in addressing the toxic behaviors; they may want to, but they don't know how.

Training workshops we lead in Dealing with Toxic Individuals, Toxic Workplaces confirm these findings.

4. **Does the power, the title, the role of the individual (high ranking or high performer) exhibiting the toxic behaviors influence how we address their actions, or if we do it all?**

"The power, the higher they are up, the more power, the more difficult it is to confront them." From an interviewee: "Drama triangle—victim, prosecutor, rescuer. Victim—person cheated on, wronged, target. Prosecutor—cheater, perpetrator, typically a powerful leader. Rescuer is HR, investigator, consultant, coach." (I found this drama triangle very helpful).

Theme: If the toxic person is making their organization a lot of money, people will look the other way. This notion of taking the bad with the profit-oriented good is very common. A big-time lawyer with a big book of business is untouchable. A very successful salesperson. We will let the toxic behavior go because they are making a lot of money for their firm.

Training workshops we lead in Dealing with Toxic Individuals, Toxic Workplaces always include case studies, situations, scenarios addressing the most powerful, executives. The devil is always in the details, step by step what to say and do.

5. **Is it that we don't know how? We lack the skills and without skills no courage or commitment.**

"In today's workplace, I am confident that organizations truly do not have the skill set to address such issues. If we look at society, our modeling, we don't have any modeling for it. For how to listen. There is also cultural decorum hardwired into us that create power separation, hierarchies that we buy into, authority figures, and we are taught not to question or piss on that live wire. Other dynamics, gender, race—complicate things."

Theme: Unanimously across all interviews, people said we lack the skills and tools. Only one interviewee said they actually provide training in their organization for these issues (having difficult conversations). It is a setup, an ambush, no one is skilled to deal with toxic issues and employers don't provide adequate training and development.

Training workshops we lead in Dealing with Toxic Individuals, Toxic Workplaces is proof that organizations need to train their personnel. They are few "naturals," and everyone can benefit from some formal training.

6. **Imagine that the person you are about to meet with is a "usual suspect," notoriously toxic behavior perpetrator. How do you prepare for the coming onslaught of negative behaviors?**

"I tell the client the truth. Simple. You prepare by being very thorough of the subject matter, know the audience and communicate in a fashion that requires closed-ended discussion. Closed-ended questions that require one-word answers as opposed to open-ended questions that would require a longer narrative has always served me well. I do not have to attend every argument in which I am invited. People will try to bait you, and it is your choice if you take the bait. Come up with what you are going to say prior to the meeting, when your mind is calm and clear. When you are not in the situation. Stay focused on facts. Establish boundaries."

Theme: Be prepared, come prepared. Know the facts, don't be emotionally hijacked by the toxic behaviors, stay focused on the pathology, the pattern of toxic behaviors and their consequences on targets and victims. Have boundaries, rules of engagement.

Training workshops we lead in Dealing with Toxic Individuals, Toxic Workplaces is all about preparing workshop participants to deal with the toxic behaviors. How to plan ahead, anticipate. To script every word of what you are going to say before you say it, to be prepared.

7. **Does your organization provide any training around dealing with toxic behaviors, having difficult conversations, and anything related?**

"Most organizations hire you and expect you to be a natural-born leader, manager, supervisor. Challenge is not that they will not provide training. Leaders don't take that training themselves."

Theme: Almost every single interviewee said there is no training provided for dealing with these issues. If provided, the people who need the training the most do not attend. I hear all the time "these are soft skills" and I always reply, "Yes, the person who calls them soft skills does not have these skills because if they did, they would know they are hard, complicated, challenging human relations, interpersonal skills."

More and more of our clients are providing this training, and we custom design the curriculum. Rare until a couple of years ago, and I think current events has played a role in this awakening, this light bulb going off for the need for this kind of training.

8. **What is your favorite tip or technique for dealing with toxic behaviors? Your most productive approach or method?**

"Own the room. Kill them with kindness (don't mirror toxicity in return). Denial and truth cannot coexist. Just be honest. Don't ignore, don't look away. Keep it in perspective. Keep yourself Zen and balanced and talk with trusted colleagues to compare notes, if they will. Write out what you will say before your meeting. Promoting open communication and active listening and fostering a culture where feedback is constructive rather than punitive. Deep breaths, meditate (prayer)."

Theme: Don't allow the toxic person to push your buttons. Don't fear them. Come prepared. Stay calm, cool, and collected. Don't let them see you sweat."

From our training: have a script written prior to any meeting or encounter.

9. **Please share with me your favorite story or memory of tangling with a toxic person and their behaviors. We will change names of people and organizations to protect their privacy.**

"When you see it, call it out. Personalities are what define places more than the work itself. Hurt people hurt people. You can't control them, but you can control how you respond."

The stories were all consistently awful people manipulating their workplaces for their own personal gain, masking their own insecurity and lack of trust for everyone around them. Many shared personal, family-oriented stories. I am always terrified when a client says "We are a like a family" because so many are dysfunctional.

All the stories in this book were presented and vetted and worked through in our workshops and these workshops are what inspired this book.

10. **Anything else you would like to add?**

"It's crucial for organizations to prioritize a culture of respect, inclusivity, and continuous improvement. Addressing toxic behaviors is a collective effort that requires ongoing commitment from leadership and team members alike. We have rules. We must be fair. It is still very much a man's world. I wait for them to slip up. Insecure people, I don't give them a fault to find."

The horror stories just poured out of my interviewees. Trauma, stress, just terrible memories of organizations not holding their toxic senior people accountable. Oh, sure, if you were lower level in an organization, they would let you go, but it is the "higher ups" who are allowed to just run all over people. These interviews were a lot of fun and cathartic, almost therapeutic for all involved.

Ultimately, it is about building a tool kit, a skill kit to empower individuals to confront, engage their toxic individuals in their lives and their behaviors. This book is all about that tool kit, skill kit. With our tool kit, skill kit, practice, and mastery, you will have the courage to battle the toxicity and win.

FURTHER LEARNING

If you want to learn more (and I believe in continuous adult learning) check out these resources.

Research Toxicity—Toxic Leaders, Toxic Managers

Top websites, articles, YouTube, TED talks, podcasts

WEBSITE/ARTICLES— ADDITIONAL RESOURCES

WEBSITES/ARTICLES:
- The Center for Respectful Leadership, https://www.respectfulleadership.org.
- 9 Key Signs of a Toxic Work Environment + Best Survival Tips by Marijana Stojanovic, in Clockify, https://clockify.me/blog/business/toxic-work-environment/.
- Study: 1 in 5 Workers Battle a Toxic Work Environment by Wellable, https://www.wellable.co/blog/study-1-in-5-workers-battle-a-toxic-work-environment/.
- Toxic Manager Behaviors—The Dark Side of Leadership by Douglas W. Bush, in LinkedIn, https://www.linkedin.com/pulse/toxic-manager-behaviors-dark-side-leadership-douglas-w-bush-m-a-/.
- Managers, Here are 6 Toxic Behaviors That Are Destroying Your Employee's Confidence by Heidi Lynn Kurter in Forbes, https://www.forbes.com/sites/heidilynnekurter/2021/07/23/managers-here-are-6-toxic-behaviors-that-are-destroying-your-employees-confidence/?sh=495b8ba46002.
- FlexJobs Report: Toxic Managers and Coworkers Pervasive in the Workplace, by Jessica Howington,

- in FlexJobs, https://www.flexjobs.com/blog/post/toxic-managers-coworkers-make-toxic-workplace/.
- 9 Signs You're in a Toxic Work Environment—and What to do About It by Puneet Sandhu in The Muse, https://www.themuse.com/advice/toxic-work-environment.
- How to Tell if a Prospective Workplace Is Toxic by Mita Mallick in Harvard Business Review, https://hbr.org/2024/01/how-to-tell-if-a-prospective-workplace-is-toxic
- The Tyranny of Toxic Managers: An Emotional Intelligence Approach to Dealing with Difficult Personalities by Roy Lubit, https://iveybusinessjournal.com/publication/the-tyranny-of-toxic-managers-an-emotional-intelligence-approach-to-dealing-with-difficult-personalities/.
- Toxic managers: A Guide for People Professionals in The Wellbeing Project, https://thewellbeingproject.co.uk/insight/toxic-managers-a-guide-for-people-professionals/.

YOUTUBES/TEDTALKS:

- Are You Navigating a Toxic Workplace? Here Is What You Can Do, by Ginny Clarke, https://www.youtube.com/watch?v=9_aO3nlSRfA.
- How to start changing an unhealthy work environment, Glenn D. Rolfsen, TEDx Talks, https://www.youtube.com/watch?v=eYLb7WUtYt8.
- Contest Culture: How Organizations Become Toxic, and How to Fix Them, Peter Glick, TEDx Talks, https://www.youtube.com/watch?v=WorAorlKeD8.

- Annie McKee Discusses Toxic Bosses by Teleos Leaders, https://www.youtube.com/watch?v=XNKJD5cuig4.

PODCASTS:

- Conflict Managed
- KimUnity Solutions Podcast
- Toxic Workplace
- Let's Break Up—Toxic Workplace Stories
- We've All Done It
- Dealing with a Difficult Boss—Livlyhood
- Breaking Bad Bosses

ACKNOWLEDGMENTS

Dr. Larry Nash and **Eric Collier**, my first mentors who put me on the path to write this book.

Shanna Heath, my first developmental editor, Shanna you are amazing and you helped me structure this book in the best way possible.

Kehkashan Khalid, my second editor, Kehkashan you added tremendous value and made this book even better with your input and insight.

Jacques Moolman, my marketing specialist, you have been so helpful and opened my eyes to so many marketing insights.

To my children, **Ethan, Elise and Maya** Velásquez, your reading and rereading of the chapters of my book were so helpful. A true family affair.

To my bride **Kelly**, for always being there for me and supporting me in this endeavor, words just can't describe how much I love you.

I want to thank my early supporters for always showing support for me in this challenging endeavor.

Heather Steranka
Andrew Bellak
Marbeth Ingle Levy
Meg Riat

Jennifer Burton

Eric Koester

I want to thank the whole Manuscripts team and their incredible process for making this book come to life. What a fabulous group of people.

NOTES

CHAPTER 1—THE TOXIC PERSON AND THEIR BEHAVIORS

1. Gretchen Livingston and Anna Brown, *Intermarriage in the US 50 Years After Loving v. Virginia* (Washington DC: Pew Research Center, 2017), https://www.pewresearch.org/social-trends/2017/05/18/intermarriage-in-the-us-50-years-after-loving-v-virginia/.
2. ADL Education Staff, "Intent vs. Impact: Why Does it Matter," (lesson plan, March 5, 2023), https://www.adl.org/resources/lesson-plan/intent-vs-impact-why-does-it-matter.
3. ADL Education Staff, "When it Comes to Bias We Must Prioritize Impact over Intent," *Anti-Defamation League's Blog* (blog), June 29, 2022, https://www.adl.org/resources/tools-and-strategies/when-it-comes-bias-we-must-prioritize-impact-over-intent.
4. Legal Information Institute, "Reasonable Person," Legal Information Institute, Cornell Law School, last modified August 2021, https://www.law.cornell.edu/wex/reasonable_person.

CHAPTER 2—HOW UNAWARE ARE YOU? NARCISSISM AT ITS BEST!

1. Psychology Today. n.d. "Narcissism." Accessed August 16, 2024, https://www.psychologytoday.com/us.
2. Donald Sull, Charles Sull, and Ben Zweig, "Toxic Culture Is Driving the Great Resignation," *Measuring Culture* (blog), *MIT Sloan Management Review*, January 11, 2022, https://sloanreview.mit.edu/article/toxic-culture-is-driving-the-great-resignation/.
3. Ibid.
4. Donald Sull, Charles Sull, and Ben Zweig, "Toxic Culture Is Driving the Great Resignation," *Measuring Culture* (blog), *MIT Sloan Management Review*, January 11, 2022, https://sloanreview.mit.edu/article/toxic-culture-is-driving-the-great-resignation/.
5. Ibid.

CHAPTER 3—ANGER MANAGEMENT, KNOW YOUR TRIGGERS

1. Kahneman, Daniel, *Thinking, Fast and Slow* (New York, NY: Farrar, Straus and Giroux, 2013).
2. Athanasios S. Drigas and Chara Papoutsi, "A New Layered Model on Emotional Intelligence," *Behavioral Sciences* 8, no. 5 (May 2018): 45, https://doi.org/10.3390/bs8050045.
3. Daniel Goleman, *Emotional Intelligence: Why It Can Matter More Than IQ* (New York, NY: Bantam Books, 2005).

CHAPTER 4—THE CEO GRABBER— DRUNK WITH POWER

1. Tasha Eurich, "What Self-Awareness Really Is (and How to Cultivate It)," *Harvard Business Review,* January 2018, https://hbr.org/2018/01/what-self-awareness-really-is-and-how-to-cultivate-it.
2. Diana Kwon, "What is Narcissism? Science Confronts a Widely Misunderstood Phenomenon." Scientific American.com, September 1, 2023, https://www.scientificamerican.com/article/what-is-narcissism-science-confronts-a-widely-misunderstood-phenomenon1/.
3. Stephen R. Covey, A. Roger Merrill, and Rebecca R. Merrill, *First Things First* (New York, NY: Free Press, 1996).

CHAPTER 5—HOME FRONT HAS BECOME MORE TOXIC

1. Julie Asher, "It's Not News that Incivility is on the Rise, but What Do We Do about It?" *The Georgia Bulletin,* December 20, 2022, https://georgiabulletin.org/news/2022/12/its-not-news-that-incivility-is-on-the-rise-but-what-do-we-do-about-it/.
2. Christine Porath, "Frontline Work When Everyone Is Angry," *Harvard Business Review,* November 2022, https://hbr.org/2022/11/frontline-work-when-everyone-is-angry.

CHAPTER 6—WORKPLACE RIDDLED WITH TOXICITY

1. Christine Porath, "Frontline Work When Everyone is Angry," *Harvard Business Review*, November 2022, https://hbr.org/2022/11/frontline-work-when-everyone-is-angry.
2. Ibid.

CHAPTER 7—FROM BYSTANDER TO UPSTANDER—IN ALL ASPECTS OF YOUR LIFE, SPORTS FOR STARTERS

1. BJ Foster, "Confronting Crazy Sports Parents," *All Pro Dad* (blog), accessed November 01, 2023, https://www.allprodad.com/confronting-crazy-sports-parents/#comment-4003745229.
2. Julianna W. Miner, "Why 70 Percent of Kids Quit Sports by Age 13," *The Washington Post*, June 1, 2016, https://www.washingtonpost.com/news/parenting/wp/2016/06/01/why-70-percent-of-kids-quit-sports-by-age-13.
3. Jennifer Newman, "It's True! Women Really Do Shop More... for Cars," *News* (blog), Cars.com, May 31, 2019, https://www.cars.com/articles/its-true-women-really-do-shop-more-for-cars-403085/.

CHAPTER 9—LIVING THE AMERICAN DREAM—SOME TOXIC FOLKS TRY TO RUIN IT

1. The Fair Housing Act of 1968, 42 U.S.C. 3601 § 1968.
2. Ibid.

CHAPTER 11—THINK LIKE A WORKPLACE INVESTIGATOR

1. Amy C. Edmondson, *The Fearless Organization: Creating Psychological Safety in the Workplace for Learning,*

Innovation, and Growth (Hoboken, NJ: John Wiley & Sons, Inc., 2018).

CHAPTER 12—GOING BACK INTO THE WORLD WITH YOUR EYES AND EARS WIDE OPEN

1. Holocaust Memorial Day Trust, "First They Came— By Pastor Martin Niemöller," *Holocaust Memorial Day Trust Blog* (blog), accessed August 27, 2024, https://www.hmd.org.uk/resource/first-they-came-by-pastor-martin-niemoller/.

www.ingramcontent.com/pod-product-compliance
Lightning Source LLC
LaVergne TN
LVHW022146141224
798956LV00041B/612